THIS AND THAT AND THE OTHER

THIS AND THAT AND THE OTHER

BY

HILAIRE BELLOC

Essay Index Reprint Series

BOOKS FOR LIBRARIES PRESS
FREEPORT, NEW YORK

First Published 1912
Reprinted 1968

INTERNATIONAL STANDARD BOOK NUMBER:
0-8369-0193-2

LIBRARY OF CONGRESS CATALOG CARD NUMBER:
68-22903

PRINTED IN THE UNITED STATES OF AMERICA

PREFACE TO THE READER

SINCE I am assured that this book requires a Preface I must attempt to write one, but I cannot conceive upon what lines it should run unless they be an apology for writing of so many things, and in very many different moods, and in so many different ways.

A Preface is intended to introduce to the Reader the air in which the book that follows must be taken, but what air attaches in common to historical reconstructions, to abstract vagaries, to stories, to jests, to the impression of a storm, and to annoyance with a dead scientist?

The sort of introduction which a book like this needs is like that which a man might find to say who should have to deliver at a house a ton of coals, some second-hand books, a warrant, several weather forecasts and a great quantity of dust. I do not know how such a man would make himself pleasant to the homestead, or prepare for the reception of so mixed a load.

But now I come to think of it the parallel is not quite just. For the man with that heap of rubbish in his cart would be bound to deliver the same, and proportionately to annoy the recipient. But you are not bound to buy, to borrow, or even to pick up this book. And even if you do you are not bound to read it. If you do read it I advise you to read the Essay beginning on page forty-five; the history beginning on page one hundred and forty-three; the denunciation of the very wickedest sort of men, which I have begun on page one hundred and three; the sort of thing which Shakespeare suffered, which you will find on page one hundred and eighty-six. When you have waded through all that you can console yourself by reading the last essay, which is intended to console you. I hope it will. Farewell.

H. BELLOC.

P.S. I have never read a Preface in my life, and I suppose you will not read this.

CONTENTS

CONTENTS

THIS AND THAT AND THE OTHER

I

AN OPEN LETTER TO A YOUNG DIPLOMATIST

My Very Dear Young Diplomatist,

My life-long friendship with your father the Old Diplomatist, must excuse me for the liberty I am now taking.

I am infinitely concerned that your career should be a successful one and that before you perish of senile decay you should have held the position of Ambassador in at least three great capitals of Europe. You certainly will not attain to such eminence unless you are early instructed by some competent authority in the mysteries of your trade, and as I am singularly well placed for giving you private information upon these, I shall immediately proceed to do so.

I beg you to remember at the very outset of your responsible profession what destinies will lie in your hands. The lives of countless inno-

1

cent men will depend upon your judgment and upon your provocation or restraint of some great war. The principal fortunes of our time will be largely dependent upon your decisions and will always fluctuate according to the advice you may give your Government. More important still, the honour of your country and its splendour before the world will hang upon your good sense and foresight. Weigh, therefore, I beg of you, before you undertake so high a function, its duties and its perils, and all that you may have to answer for at the Last Day, if indeed (as so many still pretend) human beings are answerable in the long run for the good or evil they have done upon earth. Do not, however, be deterred by any shirking of consequences, or by what Tennyson has well called " Craven fears of being great " from the tremendous task which your noble calling involves. Some one must undertake it, and why not you? Having well balanced in your mind these major things, next note carefully, I beg of you, the rules I am about to lay down.

TO A YOUNG DIPLOMATIST

The first of these is that you shall possess yourself of an income of not less than $2,000 a year. You will immediately protest, and with justice, that it is impossible upon such a revenue to impress the nobility of Austria, of Russia, or even of Montenegro, with those qualities which invariably accompany great wealth; but your objection is a youthful and improvident one. You will not be required at this outset of your activities to dazzle by any lavish expenditure the luxurious Courts of the countries I have just named. You are too young to be entrusted with any such duty and at the most it will be incumbent upon you to expend no more upon appearances than what is necessary for making a decent show at the dinner table of others. It is true that from time to time you will have to entertain at a meal, and at your own charges, a journalist perhaps or even a traveller, but from a narrow and cautious observation of some several hundred instances I have discovered that of an average of two hundred meals consumed by Young Diplomatists in the space of a year at places of public resort, no more than 83 at the most, nor less than 51 at the least, were a burden upon their purses. And by management of the simplest sort you can enjoy the hospitality of others at least three times as often as you are compelled to extend it yourself. Moreover, you will have this great advantage, that you will know the habits of the capital in which you reside and can give your guest the impression of having dined well amid luxurious surroundings, although as a matter of fact he shall have dined exceedingly ill amid surroundings which I tremble to remember: for I also have been in Arcadia.

If I have set down such a figure as $2,000 it is merely because that sum has been decided upon by those experts in the profound art of International Politics who determine the minimum for the Court of St. James.

Let us leave this sordid matter and consider next the higher part of your mission, in which connection I will first speak of what your clothing and demeanour should be.

TO A YOUNG DIPLOMATIST

It is not true that the presence of a crease clearly emphasised down the front of each trouser leg is a necessity or even an advantage to the conduct of World-wide affairs. Upon the contrary, I have come to the settled conclusion after no little review of the matter that a mere hint at such a line is not only sufficient, but preferable to any emphasis of it.

You may object to me that the eminent man who advised and all but carried out the occupation of the South Pole by the troops of Monomotapa six years ago, stretched his trousers in a machine every night, or, to speak more accurately, ordered his valet under pain of death to provide that detail. It is true. But it was not because of, it was in spite of, this habit that the Baron brought his pigs to market, and annexed to the dominion of his Sovereign those regions which were abandoned the next year with the utmost precipitation.

I yield to no one in my admiration of his amazing subtlety and comprehensive coup d'œil; but I have it upon unimpeachable testi-

5

mony that the too great rigidity of his garments formed, until the very last moment, an
obstacle to the success of his plans. I give it to
you, therefore, as a general rule, that you
should do no more than put the trousers upon
a table, and pass your hand lightly over them
before putting them on; in this way you will
produce such a crease as will suggest, and no
more than suggest, the feature upon which I
have detained you in this paragraph.

More important even than your garments will
be your method of address and in particular
your conversation with women. Here I can
only give you the advice which I fear may seem
somewhat general and vague, that you should
never neglect upon the one hand to engage in
a dialogue of some sort, nor venture, upon
the other, to be drawn into a violent alterca-
tion.

Thus, if it be your good fortune (as it was
once mine) to sit upon a marble terrace over-
looking the Mediterranean Sea, and there drink
a Chianti of that sort which the French call

TO A YOUNG DIPLOMATIST

"Iron Filings" accompanied by the flesh of goats, it would be noted disastrously against you if you refused during the whole course of the meal to utter a word to the lady upon your left or to the lady upon your right. But it will advance you in no way if at the second course you allow your ungovernable temper to become your master, and to tell either of these flanking parties what you thought of them in the heat of the moment. Any attempt to retrieve your position after such an excess by loud appeals to the justice of your cause would but degrade you further in the eyes of your chief, and you might look in vain during all succeeding years for an appointment to the conduct of important and delicate negotiations between any two great powers. No: under such circumstances (to take a concrete instance) don't mention trivial things of literature or of the weather, but discover something novel in the aspect of the sea, or recite for the advantage of the company (but at intervals of not less than five minutes) some terse falsehood that may have occurred to you, and preferably one damaging to the moral character of an innocent man.

Never contradict any statement whatsoever that may be made in your presence, at least in public. Nor, upon your part, make any affirmation which might lead to a contradiction but, after waiting until you have heard an expression of opinion from that person whom you would address, agree with it, differing only in just so much as will lend salt to the remainder of the delightful interchange. Let it appear in all you say that you are at once more learned than those about you, and yet believe them to be more learned than yourself. When you allude to the Great never do so in terms of familiarity, even if the Great be your own Uncle, but rather in terms of distant admiration or of still more distant contempt. Above all—this I most urgently charge you—confess in the most open manner a complete ignorance of how money is made, whether honourably or dishonourably. This last precept is the more difficult to fulfil when you consider that in the high-bred world of European gentlemen in which you will find yourself, money is very nearly the sole subject of discourse.

There remains to be dealt with the last exercise whereby some important mission confided to you may be brought to an issue.

I will suppose that a cautious Government is making an experiment of your abilities and has despatched you for the negotiation of a Commercial Treaty with the Viceroy of Seringapatam: a very usual test for the judging of a man's capacities.

You will, during the weeks in which sundry varlets draft letters, exchange views, consider schedules, and argue tariffs, make it your particular care to visit His Excellency and His Excellency's Wife, to play tennis with His Excellency's daughters once or twice, but more certainly to pursue in company with His Excellency's sons some animal which may be killed without any serious risk.

When the preliminaries of the Treaty have

been agreed to and the moment has come for fixing your signature thereto, it is in the essence of good breeding that you should perform the act quite simply with some ordinary pen, such for instance as the fountain pen which you carry in your pocket, and I need hardly say that jokes framed for the occasion, or any flippancy of demeanour during the solemnity would be in equally bad taste. You shall (if my memory of many such occasions serves me right) spread your left hand (which you will previously have washed very carefully) outwards over the paper, arch your eyebrows somewhat, say to your salaried friend, " Where do I sign? " and then quickly put down your name in the place indicated, and that in a very ordinary manner. These are the little things that betray not only the Gentleman but the Arbiter of the World's Destinies.

Space forbids me to deal with the minor matters of religion, affection and morals. I only beg you to keep all three under a severe restraint, and in particular the first, too great a zeal in which has early ruined many a rising young fellow.

Good-bye, my dear Young Diplomatist. If they send you to Paris ask for Berlin; and if they send you to Berlin kill yourself.

I am, in fond remembrance of your father,

Your devoted friend,

H. BELLOC.

II

ON PEDANTS

THE just and genial man will attempt to take pleasure in what surrounds him when it is capable of giving him amusement, always supposing that it does not move him to wrath. I mean, that a man who is both just and companionable will rather laugh than turn sour at the discomforts of this world. For example, consider the Pedant.

Never was such an exasperating fellow; never was there a time when he ran riot as he does now! On which account many are bewildered and many sad, they know not why, and many who know their time are soured, but a few (and I hope they may be an increasing few) are neither bewildered nor saddened nor soured by this spectacle, but claim to be made merry—and are.

What is a Pedant?

ON PEDANTS

There are many fixed human types, and every one of them has a name. There is the Priest, there is the Merchant, there is the Noble—and there is the Pedant. Each of these types are known by a distinctive name, and to most men they call up a clear image, but because they are types of mankind they are a little too complicated for definition. Nevertheless I will have a try at the Pedant.

The essence of the Pedant is twofold, first that he takes his particular science for something universal, second, that he holds with the Grip of Faith certain set phrases in that science which he has been taught. I say " with the Grip of Faith "; it is the only metaphor applicable; he has for these phrases a violent affection. Not only does he not question them, but he does not know that they can be questioned. When he repeats them it is in a fixed and hierarchic voice. When they are denied he does not answer, but flies into a passion which, were he destined to an accession of power, might in the near future turn to persecution.

13

ON PEDANTS

Alas! that the noblest thing in man should be perverted to such a use; for Faith when it is exercised upon those unprovable things which are in tune with things provable, illuminates and throws into a right perspective everything we know. But the Faith of the Pedant! . . .

The Pedant crept in upon the eclipse of our religion; his reign is therefore brief. Perhaps he is also but a reflection of that vast addition to material knowledge which glorified the last century. Perhaps it is the hurry, and the rapidity of our declining time, which makes it necessary for us to accept ready-made phrases and to act on rules of thumb good or bad. Perhaps it is the whirlpool and turmoil of classes which has pitchforked into the power of the Pedant whole groups of men who used to escape him. Perhaps it is the Devil. Whatever it is it is there.

You see it more in England than in any other European country. It runs all through the fibre of our modern literature and our modern comment, like the strings of a cancer. Come, let us have a few examples.

There is " the Anglo-Saxon race." It does not exist. It is not there. It is no more there than Baal or Moloch or the Philosopher's Stone, or the Universal Mercury. There never was any such race. There were once hundreds and hundreds of years ago a certain number of people (how many we do not know) talking a local German dialect in what is now Hampshire and Berkshire. To this dialect historians have been pleased to give the name of Anglo-Saxon, and that is all it means. If you pin your Pedant down to clear expression, saying to him, " Come, now, fellow, out with it! What is this Anglo-Saxon race of yours? " you find that he means a part (and a part only) of such people in the world as habitually speak the English language, or one of its dialects : that part only which in a muddy way he sympathises with; that part which is more or less of his religion, and more or less conformable to his own despicable self. It does not include the Irish, it does not include the negroes of the United States, but it does include a horde of German Jews, and a mixed rabble of every origin under the sun sweating in the slums of the New World.

Why then you may ask, and you may well ask, does the man use the phrase "Anglo-Saxon" at all?

The answer is simple. It smacks—or did originally smack—of learning. Among the innumerable factors of modern Europe one, and only one, was the invasion of the Eastern part of this island (and only the Eastern part) by pirates from beyond the North Sea. The most of these pirates (but by no means all) belonged either to a loose conglomeration of tribes whom the Romans called Saxones, or to a little maritime tribe called Angles. True, the full knowledge of that event is a worthy subject of study; there is a good week's reading upon it in original authorities, and I can imagine a conscientious man who would read slowly and make notes, spending a fortnight upon the half dozen contemporary sources of knowledge we possess upon these little barbarian peoples. But, Lord! what a superstructure the Pedant has raised upon that narrow base!

Then there is " alcohol "; what " alcohol " does to the human body, and the rest of it; to read the absurd fellows one would imagine that this stuff " alcohol " was something you could see and handle; something with which humanity was familiar, like Beef, Oak, Sand, Chalk, and the rest. Not a bit of it. It does not exist any more than the " Anglo-Saxon race " exists. It is a chemical extraction. And in connection with it you have something very common to all such folly, to wit, gross insufficiency even in the line to which its pedantry is devoted. For this chemical abstraction of theirs may be expressed in many forms and it is only in one of these forms that they mouth out their interminable and pretentious dogmas. Humanity, healthy European humanity that is, the jolly place called Christendom, has drunk from immemorial time wine and beer and cider. It has been noticed (also from immemorial time) that

17

if a man drank too much of any of these things he got drunk, and that if he got drunk often his health and capacity declined. There is the important fact which humanity has never missed, and without which the rhodomontades of the Pedant would have no foothold. It is because his pretended knowledge relates to a real evil with which humanity is acquainted that people listen to him at all on the subject. He ill requites their confidence! He exploits and bamboozles them to the top of their bent. He terrifies the weak victims (and the weaker witnesses) of drunkenness and often, I am sorry to say, picks their pockets as well. I can call to mind as I write more than one Pedant who by harping on this word " alcohol " has got very considerable sums out of the public. Well, it is the public's fault! *Vult decipi et decipiatur.* And a murrain on it—also a quinsy!

Then there is " the Fourth Gospel ": your Pedant never calls it the Gospel of S. John, as his fathers have done before him for two thousand years. He must give it a pretentious name and then, because it happens to be cram-full of Christian doctrine, he must deny its authenticity. There is not a vestige of proof against that authenticity, nor for that matter a vestige of sound historical proof in favour of it. Like everything else in the fundamental structure of the Faith from the Mass to the Apocalypse, it has for witness the tradition of the Church, and is no more acceptable as an historic document of the type of the "Agricola" or the "Catiline Orations" than any one of the other Gospels. There is not an event mentioned in the whole of the New Testament which has true historic value. The whole thing depends upon Belief, and Belief in a corporate teaching body. Yet how your Pedant has flourished upon this same Fourth Gospel! Now he is "reverently accepting it," now "reluctantly rejecting it"; he fondles it as a cat does a mouse, and when you try to come to handgrips with him he will first (taking you for a simple and unlearned man) put you off with silly technicalities. You have but to read up the meaning of these tech-

19

nicalities in the dictionary to find that he is talking through his hat. He has no evidence, and there can be no evidence, as to whether the Gospel was or was not written by the traditional figure which the Catholic Church calls S. John, and all he has to say on the matter would not tempt the most gullible gambler to invest a penny on a ten-to-one chance.

Then there is " the conflict between religion and science." What the Pedant really means when he uses that phrase (and he has not only used it threadbare but has fed it by the ton to the recently enfranchised and to the vulgar in general) is the conflict between a mystical doctrine and every-day common sense. That conflict has always existed and always will exist. If you say to any man who has not heard of such a thing before " I will kill you and yet you will survive " or " This water is not ordinary water, it does more than wash you or assuage your thirst, it will also cure blindness, and make whole a diseased limb," the man who has not heard such things before, will call you a liar;

of course he will, and small blame to him. We can only generalise from repeated experience, and oddities and transcendental things are not within the field of repeated experience. But " science " has nothing to do with that. The very fact that they use the word religion is enough to show the deplorable insufficiency of their minds. What religion? Your Pedant is far too warped and hypocritical to say exactly what he means even in so simple a case; so he uses the word " religion," a term which may apply to Thugs with their doctrine of the sanctity of murder, or to the Mahommedans who are not bound to any transcendental doctrine but only to a Rule of Life, or to Buddhists who have but a philosophy, or to Plymouth Brethren, or to Head Hunters.

I said at the beginning of this that the Pedant was food for laughter, rather than for anger.

Humph!

III

ON ATHEISM

THE Atheist is he that has forgotten God.   He
that denies God may do so in many innocent
ways, and is an Atheist in form, but is not con-
demnable as such.   Thus one man will reason
by contradiction that there can be no God.
If there were a God (says he), how could
such things be?   This man has not read or
does not know sufficient to his purpose, or is
not wide enough.   His purpose is Truth, so he
is not to be condemned.   Another will say,
" There is no God," meaning, " There is none
that I have heard called God ": as, the figure
of an old man; some vengeful spirit; an ab-
surdity taught him by fools; and so forth.
Another also will say, " There is no God," as
he would say, " Thus do I solve this riddle! "
He has played a game, coming to a conclusion
of logic, and supposes himself right by the

rules of the game. Nor is he more to be condemned than one who shall prove, not that God is not, but that God is, by similar ways. For though this last man proves truth, and that first man falsehood, yet each is only concerned with proving, and not with making good or standing up for the Truth, so that it shall be established. Neither would found in the mind something unshakeable, but each would rather bring a process to its conclusion for neatness.

We call that man Atheist who, thinking or unthinking, waking or sleeping, knows not God; and when it is brought to him that either God is not or is, would act as though the question mattered nothing. Such an Atheist makes nothing of God's judgments nor of his commands. He does not despise them but will have them absent, as he will have God absent also. Nor is he a rebel but rather an absconder.

Of Atheism you may see that it is proper to a society and not to a man, so that Atheists are proper to an Atheist Commonwealth, and this because we find God in mankind or lose him there.

Rousseau would have no Atheist in the Republic. All other opinion he thought tolerable, but this intolerable because through it was loosened every civil bond. But if a Commonwealth be not Atheist no Atheist will be within it, since it is through men and their society that one man admits God. No one quite lonely could understand or judge whether of God's existence or of much lesser things. A man quite lonely could not but die long before he was a man grown. He would have no speech or reason. Also a man Atheist in a Commonwealth truly worshipping would be abhorrent as a traitor with us and would stand silent. How, then, would Rousseau not tolerate the Atheist in his Republic, seeing that if his Republic were not Atheist no Atheist could be therein? Of this contradiction the solution is that false doctrine of any kind is partially hidden and striving in the minds of men before one man shall become its spokesman. Now of false doctrine when it is thus blind and under water nothing can be either tolerated or proscribed. The ill-ease of it is felt but no magistrate can seize it anywhere. But when one man brings it up to reason and arms it with words, then has it been born (as it were) into the world, and can be tried and judged, accepted or expelled.

No Commonwealth has long stood that was Atheist, yet many have been Atheist a little before they died: as some men lose the savour of meats, and the colours and sounds of things also a little before they die.

A Commonwealth fallen into this palsy sees no merit in God's effect of Justice, but makes a game of law. In peril, as in battle or shipwreck, each man will save himself. In commerce man will cozen man. The Commonwealth grown Atheist lets the larger prey upon the less, until all are eaten up.

They say that a man not having seen salt or knowing that such a thing as salt might be and even denying that salt could be (since he had not seen it), might yet very livelily taste the saltness of the sea. So it is with men who still love Justice, though they have lost Religion. For these men are angered by evil-doing, and will risk their bodies in pity and in indignation. They therefore truly serve God in whose essence Justice resides, and of whom the Effect in Society is Justice. But what shall we say of a man who speaks of salt as a thing well known, and yet finds no division between his well and the water of the sea? And that is the Atheist case. When men of a mean sinfulness purchase a seat of judgment, and therein, while using the word " God," care nothing for right but consider the advantage of their aged limbs and bellies, or of the fellow rich they drink with, then they are Atheist indeed.

That Commonwealth also is Atheist in which the rulers will use the fear of God for a cheat, hoping thereby to make foolish men work for them, or give up their goods, or accept insult and tyranny. It is so ordered that this trick most powerfully slings back upon its authors, and that the populace are now moved at last not by empty sentences which have God's name in them, but by lively devils. In the end of such cheats the rich men who so lied are murdered and by a side wind God comes to his own.

One came to a Courtier who had risen high in the State by flattery and cowardice, but who had a keen wit. To this Courtier he propounded a certain scheme which would betray the Commonwealth, and this the Courtier agreed to. But when he had done so he said: " Either God is or is not. If he is not, why then we have chosen well."

This instance is a mark and Atheism is judged by it. For if God is not, then all falsehoods, though each prove the rest false, are each true, and every evil is its own good, and there is confusion everywhere. But if God is, then the world can stand. Now that the world does stand all men know and live by, even those who, not in a form of words but in the heart, deny its Grand Principle.

IV

ON FAME

FAME is that repute among men which gives us pleasure. It needs much repetition, but also that repetition honourable. Of all things desired Fame least fulfils the desire for it; for if Fame is to be very great a man must be dead before it is more than a shoot; he therefore has not the enjoyment of it (as it would seem). Again, Fame while a man lives is always tarnished by falsehood; for since few can observe him, and less know him, he must have Fame for work which he does not do and forego Fame for work which he knows deserves it.

Fame has no proper ending to it, when it is first begun, as have things belonging to other appetites, nor is any man satiated with it at any time. Upon the contrary, the hunger after it will lead a man forward madly always to some sort of disaster, whether of disappointment in the soul, or of open dishonour.

Fame is not to be despised or trodden under as a thing not to be sought, for no man is free of the desire of it, nor can any man believe that desire to be an imperfection in him unless he desire at the same time something greater than Fame, and even then there is a flavour of Fame certain to attach to his achievement in the greater thing. No one can say of Fame, " I contemn it " ; as a man can say of titles, " I contemn them." Nor can any man say of the love of Fame, " This is a thing I should cast from me as evil," as a man may say of lust when it is inordinate, that is, out of place. Nor can any man say of Fame, " It is a little thing," for if he says that he is less or more than a man.

The love of Fame is the mobile of all great work in which also man is in the image of God, who not only created but took pleasure in what he did and, as we know, is satisfied by praise thereof.

In what way, then, shall men treat Fame?

ON FAME

How shall they seek it, or hope to use it if obtained? To these questions it is best answered that a man should have for Fame a natural appetite, not forced nor curiously entertained; it must be present in him if he would do noble things. Yet if he makes the Fame of those things, and not those things themselves his chief business, then not only will he pursue Fame to his hurt, but also Fame will miss him. Though he should not disregard it yet he must not pursue it to himself too much, but he will rightly make of it in difficult times a great consolation.

When Fame comes upon a man well before death then must he most particularly beware of it, for is it then most dangerous. Neither must he, having achieved it, relax effort nor (a much greater peril) think he has done his work because some Fame now attaches thereto.

Some say that after a man has died the spreading of his earthly Fame is still a pleasure to him among greater scenes: but this is doubtful. One thing is certain, Fame is enjoyable in good things accomplished; bitter, noisome and poisonous in all other things—whether it be the Fame of things thought to be accomplished but not accomplished, or Fame got by accident, or Fame for evil things concealed because they are evil.

The judgment of Fame is this: That many men having done great things of a good sort have not Fame. And that many men have Fame who have done but little things and most of them evil. The virtue of Fame is that it nourishes endeavour. The peril of Fame is that it leads men towards itself, and therefore into inanities and sheer loss. But Fame has a fruit, which is a sort of satisfaction coming from our communion with mankind.

They that believe they deserve Fame though they lack it may be consoled in this: that soon they shall be concerned with much more lasting things, and things more immediate and more true: just as a man who misses some entertainment at a show will console himself if he knows that shortly he shall meet his love. They that

ON FAME

have Fame may correct its extravagances by the
same token: remembering that shortly they will
be so occupied that this earthly Fame of theirs
will seem a toy.   Old men know this well.

V

ON REST

REST is not the conclusion of labour but the recreation of power. It seems a reward because it fulfils a need: but that need being filled, Rest is but an extinction and a nothingness. So we do not pray for Rest; but (in a just religion) we pray after this life for refreshment, light and peace—not for Rest.

Rest is only for a little while, as also is labour only for a little while: each demanding the other as a supplement; yet is Rest in some intervals a necessary ground for seed, and without Rest to protect the sprouting of the seed no good thing ever grew.

Of many follies in a Commonwealth concerning Rest the chief is that Rest is not needed for all effort therein. Thus one man at leisure will obtain work of another for many days without a sufficiency of Rest for that other and think

to profit by this. So he may: but he profits
singly, and when many rich do so by the poor
it is like one eating his own flesh, since the
withdrawal of Rest from those that labour will
soon eat up the Commonwealth itself.

Much that men do with most anxiety is for
the establishment of Rest. Wise men have
often ordered gardens carefully for years, in
order to enjoy Rest at last. Beds also are de-
vised best when they give the deepest interval of
repose and are surrounded by artifice with prolonged silence, made of quiet strong wood and
well curtained from the morning light. It is so
with rooms removed from the other rooms
of a house, and with days set apart from
labour, and with certain kinds of companionship.

Undoubtedly the regimen of Rest for men is
that of sleep, and sleep is a sort of medicine to
Rest, and again a true expression of it. For
though these two, Rest and Sleep, are not the
same yet without sleep no man can think of
Rest nor has Rest any one better body or way

of being than this thing Sleep. For in sleep a man utterly sinks down in proportion as it is deep and good into the centre of things and becomes one with that from which he came, drawing strength not only by negation from repose, but in some way positive from the being of his mother which is the earth. Some say that sleep is better near against the ground on this account and all men know that sleep in wild places and without cover is the surest and the best. Sleep promises waking as Rest does a renewal of power; and the good dreams that come to us in sleep are a proof that in sleep we are still living.

A man may deny himself any other voluptuousness but not Rest. He may forego wine or flesh or anything of the body, and music or disputation, or anything of the mind, or love itself, or even companionship; but not Rest, for if he denies himself this he wastes himself and is himself no longer. Rest, therefore, is a necessary intermittent which we must have both for soul and body and is the only necessity inherent to both those two so long as those two are bound together in the matter and net of this world. For food is a necessity to the body and virtue to the soul, but Rest to one and to the other.

There is no picture of delight in which we envy other men so much as when, lacking Rest, we see them possessing it; on which occasions we call out unwisely for a Perpetual Rest and for the cessation of all endeavour. In the same way men devise a lack of Rest for a special torment, and none can long survive it.

Rest and innocence are good fellows, and Rest is easier to the innocent man. The wicked suffer unrest always in some sort on account of God's presence warning them, though this unrest is stronger and much more to their good if men also warn them and if they live among such fellows in their commonwealth as will not permit their wickedness to be hidden or to go unpunished.

Rest has no time, and in its perfection must lose all mark of time. So a man sleeping deeply knows not how many hours have passed since he fell asleep until he awake again.

There are many good accompaniments for Rest, slow and distant music which at last is stiller and then silent; the scent of certain herbs and flowers and particularly of roses; clean linen; a pure clear air and the coming of night. To all these things prayer, an honourable profession and a preparation of the mind are in general a great aid, and, in the heat of the season, cool water refreshed with essences. A man also should make his toilet for Rest if he would have it full and thorough and prepare his body as his soul for a relaxation. He does well also in the last passage of his mind into sleep to commend himself to the care of God; remembering both how petty are all human vexations and also how weathercock they are, turning now a face of terror and then in a moment another face of laughter or of insignificance. Many troubles that seem giants at evening are but dwarfs at sunrise, and some most terrific prove ghosts which speed off with the broadening of the day.

37

VI

ON DISCOVERY

THERE is a great consolation lying all bottled and matured for those who choose to take it, in the modern world—and yet hrw few turn to it and drink the bracing draft! It is a consolation for dust and frequency and fatigue and despair—this consolation is the Discovery of the World.

The world has no end to it. You can discover one town which you had thought well known, or one quarter of the town, or one house in the quarter of the town, or one room in that house, or one picture in that room. The avenues of discovery open out infinite in number and quite a little distance from their centre (which is yourself and your local, tired, repeated experience) these avenues diverge outwards and lead to the most amazingly different things.

ON DISCOVERY

You can take some place of which you have heard so often and in so vulgar a connotation that you could wish never to hear of it again, and coming there you will find it holding you, and you will enjoy many happy surprises, unveiling things you could not dream were there.

How much more true is it not, then, that discovery awaits you if you will take the least little step off the high road, or the least little exploration into the past of a place you visit.

Most men inhabiting a countryside know nothing of its aspect even quite close to their homes, save as it is seen from the main roads. If they will but cross a couple of fields or so, they may come, for the first time in many years of habitation, upon a landscape that seems quite new and a sight of their own hills which makes them look like the hills of a strange country.

In youth we all know this. In youth and early manhood we wonder what is behind some rise of land, or on the other side of some wood which bounded our horizon in childhood. Then

comes a day when we manfully explore the unknown places and go to find what we shall find.

As life advances we imagine that all this
chance of discovery has been taken from us
by our increased experience. It is an illusion.
If we are so dull it is we that have changed
and not the world; and what is more we can
recover from that dulness, and there is a simple medicine for it, which is to repeat the old
experiment: to go out and see what we may see.

Some will grant this true of the sudden little
new discoveries quite close to home, but not
of travel. Travel, they think, must always be
to-day by some known road to some known
place, with dust upon the mind at the setting
out and at the coming in. It is a great error.
You can choose some place too famous in
Europe and even too peopled and too large, and
yet make the most ample discoveries there.

" Oh, but," a man will say, " most places have
been so written of that one knows them already
long before seeing them."

No: one does nothing of the kind. Even

the pictured and the storied places are full enough of newness if one will but shake off routine and if one will but peer.

Speak to five men of some place which they have all visited, perhaps together, and find out what each noticed most: you will be amazed at the five different impressions.

Enter by some new entry a town which hitherto you had always entered by one fixed way, and again vary your entry, and again, and you will see a new town every time.

There are many, many thousand Englishmen who know the wonderful sight of Rouen from the railway bridge below the town, for that lies on the high road to Paris, and there are many thousand, though not so many, who know Rouen from Bon-Secours. There are a few hundred who know it from the approach by the great woods to the North. There are a dozen or so perhaps who have come in from the East, walking from Picardy. The great town lying in its cup of hills is quite different every way.

ON DISCOVERY

There is a view of Naples which has been photographed and printed and painted until we are all tired of it. It is a view taken from the hill which makes the northern horn of the Bay; there is a big pine tree in the foreground and Vesuvius smoking in the background, and I will bargain that most people who read this have seen that view upon a postcard, or in a shop window, and that a good many of them would rightly say that it was the most hackneyed thing in Europe.

Now some years ago I had occasion to go to Naples, a town I had always avoided for that very reason—that one heard of it until one was tired and that this view had become like last year's music-hall tunes.

I went, not of my own choice but because I had to go, and when I got there I made as complete a discovery as ever Columbus made or those sailors who first rounded Africa and found the Indian Seas.

Naples was utterly unlike anything I had imagined. Vesuvius was not a cone smoking upon the horizon—it was a great angry pyramid toppling right above me. The town was not a lazy, dirty town with all the marks of antiquity and none of energy. It was alive with commerce and all the evils and all the good of commerce. It was angrily alive; it was like a wasp nest.

I will state the plain truth at the risk of being thought paradoxical. Naples recalled to me an *American* seaboard town so vividly that I could have thought myself upon the Pacific. I could have gone on for days digging into all this new experience, turning it over and fructifying it. My business allowed me not twenty-four hours, but the vision was one I shall never forget, and it was as completely new and as wholly creative, or re-creative, of the mind, as is that land-fall which an adventurous sailor makes when he finds a new island at dawn upon a sea not yet travelled.

Every one, therefore, should go out to discover, five miles from home, or five hundred.

43

ON DISCOVERY

Every one should assure himself against the cheating tedium which books and maps create in us, that the world is perpetually new: and oddly enough it is not a matter of money.

VII

ON INNS

HERE am I sitting in an Inn, having gloomily believed not half an hour ago that Inns were doomed with all other good things, but now more hopeful 'and catching avenues of escape through the encircling decay.

For though certainly that very subtle and final expression of a good nation's life, the Inn, is in peril, yet possibly it may survive.

This Inn which surrounds me as I write (the law forbids me to tell its name) is of the noblest in South England, and it is in South England that the chief Inns of the world still stand. In the hall of it, as you come in, are barrels of cider standing upon chairs. The woman that keeps this Inn is real and kind. She receives you so that you are glad to enter the house. She takes pleasure in her life. What was her beauty her daughter now inherits, and she serves at the bar. Her son is strong and carries up the luggage. The whole place is a paradise, and as one enters that hall one stands hesitating whether to enjoy its full, yet remaining delight, or to consider the peril of death that hangs to-day over all good things.

Consider, you wanderers (that is all men, whatsoever, for not one of you can rest), what an Inn is, and see if it should not rightly raise both great fears and great affection.

An Inn is of the nation that made it. If you desire a proof that the unity of Christendom is not to be achieved save through a dozen varying nations, each of a hundred varying counties and provinces and these each of several countrysides—the Inns will furnish you with that proof.

If any foolish man pretend in your presence that the brotherhood of men should make a decent man cosmopolitan, reprove his error by the example of an Inn.

If any one is so vile as to maintain in your presence that one's country should not be loved and loyally defended, confound so horrid a fool by the very vigorous picture of an Inn. And if he impudently says that some damned Babylon or other is better than an Inn, look up his ancestry.

For the truth is that Inns (may God preserve them, and of the few remaining breed, in spite of peril, a host of new Inns for our sons), Inns, Inns are the mirror and at the same time the flower of a people. The savour of men met in kindliness and in a homely way for years and years comes to inhabit all their panels (Inns are panelled) and lends incense to their fires. (Inns have not radiators, but fires.) But this good quintessence and distillation of comradeship varies from countryside to countryside and more from province to province, and more still from race to race and from realm to realm; just as speech differs and music and all the other excellent fruits of Europe.

Thus there is an Inn at Tout-de-suite-Tardets which the Basques made for themselves and offer to those who visit their delightful streams.

ON INNS

A river flows under its balcony, tinkling along a sheer stone wall, and before it, high against the sunset, is a wood called Tiger Wood, clothing a rocky peak called the Peak of Eagles.

Now no one could have built that Inn nor endowed it with its admirable spirit, save the cleanly but incomprehensible *Basques.* There is no such Inn in the Béarnese country, nor any among the Gascons.

In Falaise the Normans very slowly and by a mellow process of some thousand years have engendered an Inn. This Inn, I think, is so good that you will with difficulty compare it with any better thing. It is as quiet as a tree on a summer night, and cooks crayfish in an admirable way. Yet could not these *Normans* have built that *Basque* Inn; and a man that would merge one in the other and so drown both is an outlaw and to be treated as such.

But these Inns of South England (such as still stand!)—what can be said in proper praise of them which shall give their smell and colour and their souls? There is nothing like them in Europe, nor anything to set above them in all the world. It is within their walls and at their boards that one knows what South England once did in the world and why. If it is gone it is gone. All things die at last. But if it *is* gone—why, no lover of it need remain to drag his time out in mourning it. If South England is dead it is better to die upon its grave.

Whether it dies in our time or no you may test by the test of its *Inns.* If they may not weather the chaos, if they fail to round the point that menaces our religion and our very food, our humour and our prime affections— why, then, South England has gone too. If, if (I hardly dare to write such a challenge), if the Inns hold out a little time longer—why, then, South England will have turned the corner and Europe can breathe again. Never mind her extravagances, her follies or her sins. Next time you see her from a hill, pray for South England. For if she dies, you die. And as a symptom of her malady (some would say of her death-throes) carefully watch her Inns.

49

Of the enemies of Inns, as of rich men, dull men, blind men, weak-stomached men and men false to themselves, I do not speak: but of their effect. Why such blighting men are nowadays so powerful and why God have given them a brief moment of pride it is not for us to know. It is hidden among the secret things of this life. But that they *are* powerful all men, lovers of Inns, that is, lovers of right living, know well enough and bitterly deplore. The effect of their power concerns us. It is like a wasting of our own flesh, a whitening of our own blood.

Thus there is the destruction of an Inn by gluttony of an evil sort—though to say so sounds absurd, for one would imagine that gluttony should be proper to Inns. And so it is, when it is your true gluttony of old, the gluttony of our fathers made famous in English letters by the song which begins:

I am not a glutton
But I do like pie.

But evil gluttony, which may also be called

the gluttony of devils, is another matter. It flies to liquor as to a drug; it is ashamed of itself; it swallows a glass behind a screen and hides. There is no companionship with it. It is an abomination, and this abomination has the power to destroy a Christian Inn and to substitute for it, first a gin-palace, and then, in reaction against that, the very horrible house where they sell only tea and coffee and bubbly waters that bite and sting both in the mouth and in the stomach. These places are hotbeds of despair, and suicides have passed their last hours on earth consuming slops therein alone.

Thus, again, a sad enemy of Inns is luxury. The rich will have their special habitations in a town so cut off from ordinary human beings that no Inn may be built in their neighbourhood. In which connection I greatly praise that little colony of the rich which is settled on the western side of Berkeley Square, in Lansdowne House, and all around the eastern parts of Charles Street, for they have per-

mitted to be established in their midst the
" Running Footman," and this will count in
the scale when their detestable vices are weighed
upon the Day of Judgment, upon which day,
you must know, vices are not put into the scale
gently and carefully so as to give you fair
measure, but are banged down with enormous
force by strong and maleficent demons.

Then, again, a very subtle enemy of Inns is
poverty, when it is pushed to inhuman limits,
and you will note especially in the dreadful
great towns of the North, more than one ancient house which was once honourable and
where Mr. Pickwick might very well have stayed,
now turned ramshackle and dilapidated and
abandoned, slattern, draggle-tail, a blotch, until
the yet beastlier reformers come and pull it
down to make an open space wherein the stunted
children may play.

Thus, again, you will have the pulling down
of an Inn and the setting up of an Hotel built
of iron and mud, or ferro-concrete. This is
murder.

ON INNS

Let me not be misunderstood. Many an honest Inn calls itself an hotel. I have no quarrel with that, nor has any traveller I think. It is a title. Some few blighted and accursed hotels call themselves " Inns "—a foul snobbism, a nasty trick of words pretending to create realities.

No, it is when the thing is really done, not when the name is changed that murder calls out to God for vengeance.

I knew an Inn in South England, when I was a boy, that stood on the fringe of a larch wood, upon a great high road. Here when the springtime came and I went off to see the world I used to meet with carters and with travelling men, also keepers and men who bred horses and sold them, and sometimes with sailors padding the hoof between port and port. These men would tell me a thousand things. The larch trees were pleasant in their new colour; the woods alive with birds and the great high road was, in those days, deserted: for high bicycles were very rare, low bicycles were not invented, the rich went by train in those days; only carts and caravans and men with horses used the leisurely surface of the way.

Now that good Inn has gone. I was in it some five years ago, marvelling that it had changed so little, though motor things and money-changers went howling by in a stream and though there were now no poachers or gipsies or forestmen to speak to, when a too smart young man came in with two assistants and they began measuring, calculating, two-foot-ruling and jotting. This was the plot. Next came the deed. For in another year, when the Spring burst and I passed by, what should I see in the place of my Inn, my Inn of youth, my Inn of memories, my Inn of trees, but a damnable stack of iron with men fitting a thin shell of bricks to it like a skin. Next year the monster was alive and made. The old name (call it the Jolly) was flaunting on a vulgar signboard swing in cast-iron tracing to imitate forged work. The shell of bricks was cast with sham white as for half-timber work. The sham-white was patterned with sham timbers of baltic deal, stained dark, with pins of wood stuck in: like Cheshire, not like home. Wrong lattice insulted the windows—and inside there were three bars. At the door stood an Evil Spirit, and within every room upstairs and down other devils, his servants, resided.

It is no light thing that such things should be done and that we cannot prevent them.

From the towns all Inns have been driven: from the villages most. No conscious efforts, no Bond Street nastiness of false conservation, will save the beloved roofs. Change your hearts or you will lose your Inns and you will deserve to have lost them. But when you have lost your Inns drown your empty selves, for you will have lost the last of England.

VIII

ON ROWS

THE HON. MEMBER: *Mr. Speaker, Mr. Speaker! Is the Hon. Member in order in calling me an insolent swine?*

(*See Hansard passim*)

A DISTINGUISHED literary man has composed and perhaps will shortly publish a valuable poem the refrain of which is " I like the sound of broken glass."

This concrete instance admirably illustrates one of the most profound of human appetites: indeed, an appetite which, to the male half of humanity, is more than an appetite and is, rather, a necessity: the appetite for rows.

It has been remarked by authorities so distant and distinct, yet each so commanding, as Aristotle and Confucius, that words lose their meanings in the decline of a State.

ON ROWS

Absolutely purposeless phrases go the rounds, are mechanically repeated; sometimes there is an attempt by the less lively citizens to *act* upon such phrases when Society is diseased! And so to-day you have the suburban fool who denounces the row. Sometimes he calls it ungentlemanly—that is, unsuitable to the wealthy male. If he says *that* he simply cannot know what he is talking about.

If there is one class in the community which has made more rows than another it is the young male of the wealthier classes, from Alcibiades to my Lord Tit-up. When men are well fed, good-natured, fairly innocent (as are our youth) then rows are their meat and drink. Nay, the younger males of the gentry have such a craving and necessity for a row that they may be observed at the universities of this country making rows continually without any sort of object or goal attached to such rows.

Sometimes he does not call it ungentlemanly, but points out that a row is of no effect, by which he means that there is no money in it.

That is true, neither is there money in drinking, or breathing, or sleeping, but they are all very necessary things. Sometimes the row is denounced by the suburban gentleman as unchristian; but that is because he knows nothing about human history or the Faith, and plasters the phrase down as a label without consideration. The whole history of Christendom is one great row. From time to time the Christians would leap up and swarm like bees, making the most hideous noise and pouring out by millions to whang in their Christianity for as long as it could be borne upon the vile persons of the infidel. More commonly the Christians would vent their happy rage one against the other.

The row is better fun when it is played according to rule: it sounds paradoxical, and your superficial man might conceive that the essence of a row was anarchy. If he did he would be quite wrong; a row being a male thing at once demands all sorts of rules and complications. Otherwise it would be no fun. Take, for instance, the oldest and most solid of our national

rows—the House of Commons row. Everybody
knows how it is done and everybody surely
knows that very special rules are observed. For
instance, there is the word " traitor." That is
in order. It was decided long ago, when Mr.
Joseph Chamberlain, of Birmingham, called Mr.
Dillon a traitor. But I have heard with my
own ears the word " party-hack " ruled out.
It is not allowed.

By a very interesting decision of the Chair,
pointing is ruled out also. If a member of the
House suddenly thrusts out his arm with a long
forefinger at the end of it and directs this instrument towards some other member, the Chair
has decided the gesture to be out of order. It
is, as another member of the Chamberlain family has said, " No class." Throwing things is
absolutely barred. Nor may you now imitate
the noise of animals in the chamber itself. This
last is a recent decision, or rather it is an example of an old practice falling into desuetude.
The last time a characteristic animal cry was
heard in the House of Commons was when a

very distinguished lawyer, later Lord Chief
Justice of England, gave an excellent render-
ing of a cock-crow behind the Speaker's chair
during a difference of opinion upon the matter
of Home Rule—but this was more than twenty
years ago.

It is a curious thing that Englishmen no
longer sing during their rows. The fine song
about the House of Lords which had a curse
in it and was sung some months ago by two
drunken men in Pall Mall to the lasting pleasure
of the clubs, would come in very well at this
juncture; or that other old political song now
forgotten, the chorus of which is (if my memory
serves me), " Bow wow wow!"

No one has seized the appetite for a row
more fully than the ladies who demand the
suffrage. The " disgraceful scenes " and " un-
womanly conduct " which we have all heard
officially denounced, were certainly odd, proceeding as they did from great groups of
middle-class women as unsuited to exercises of
this sort as a cow would be to following hounds,

but there is no doubt that the men enjoyed it hugely. It had all the fun of a good football scrimmage about it, except when they scratched. And to their honour be it said they did not stab with those murderous long pins about which the Americans make so many jokes.

Before leaving this fascinating subject of rows, we will draw up for the warning of the reader a list of those to whom rows are abhorrent. Luckily they are few. Money-lenders dislike rows; political wire-pullers dislike rows; very tired men recovering from fevers must be put in the same category, and, finally, oddly enough, newspaper proprietors.

Why on earth this last little band—there are not a couple of dozen of them that count in the country—should have such a feature in common, Heaven only knows, but they most undoubtedly have; and they compel their unfortunate employees to write on the subject of rows most amazing and incomprehensible nonsense. There is no accounting for tastes!

IX

THE PLEASANT PLACE

A GENTLEMAN of my acquaintance came to me the other day for sympathy. . . . But first I must describe him:—

He is a man of careful, not neat, dress: I would call it sober rather than neat. He is always clean-shaven and his scanty hair is kept short-cut. He is occupied in letters; he is, to put it bluntly, a litteratoor; none the less he is possessed of scholarship and is a minor authority upon English pottery.

He is a very good writer of verse; he is not exactly a poet, but still, his verse is remarkable. Two of his pieces have been publicly praised by political peers and at least half a dozen of them have been praised in private by the ladies of that world. He is a man fifty-four years of age, and, if I may say so without betraying him, a little disappointed.

62

THE PLEASANT PLACE

He came to me, I say, for sympathy. I was sitting in my study watching the pouring rain falling upon the already soaked and drenched and drowned clay lands of my county. The leafless trees (which are in our part of a low but thick sort) were standing against a dead grey sky with a sort of ghost of movement in it, when he came in, opened his umbrella carefully so that it might not drip, and left it in the stone-floored passage—which is, to be accurate, six hundred years old—kicked off his galoshes and begged my hospitality; also (let me say it for the third time) my sympathy.

He said he had suffered greatly and that he desired to tell me the whole tale. I was very willing, and his tale was this:

It seems that my friend (according to his account) found himself recently in a country of a very delightful character.

This country lay up and heavenly upon a sort of table-land. One went up a road which led continually higher and higher through the ravines of the mountains, until, passing through a natural gate of rock, one saw before one a wide plain bounded upon the further side by the highest crests of the range. Through this upland plain ran a broad and noble river whose reaches he could see in glimpses for miles, and upon the further bank of it in a direction opposite that which the gate of rock regarded, was a very delightful city.

The walls of this city were old in their texture, venerable and majestic in their lines. Within their circumference could be discerned sacred buildings of a similar antiquity, but also modern and convenient houses of a kind which my friend had not come across before, but which were evidently suited to the genial, sunlit climate, as also to the habits of leisured men. Their roofs were flat, covered in places by awnings, in other places by tiled verandas, and these roofs were often disposed in the form of little gardens.

Trees were numerous in the city and showed their tops above the lower buildings, while the lines of their foliage indicated the direction of the streets.

THE PLEASANT PLACE

My friend was passing down the road which led to this plain—and as it descended it took on an ampler and more majestic character—when he came upon a traveller who appeared to be walking in the direction of the town.

This traveller asked him courteously in the English tongue whether he were bound for the city. My friend was constrained to reply that he could not pretend to any definite plan, but certainly the prospect all round him was so pleasant and the aspect of the town so inviting, that he would rather visit the capital of this delightful land at once than linger in its outskirts.

"Come with me, then," said the Traveller, "and if I may make so bold upon so short an acquaintance, accept my hospitality. I have a good house upon the wall of the town and my rank among the citizens of it is that of a merchant;—I am glad to say a prosperous one."

He spoke without affectation and with so much kindness, that my friend was ravished to discover such a companion, and they proceeded in leisurely company over the few miles that separated them from their goal.

The road was now paved in every part with small square slabs, quite smooth and apparently constructed of some sort of marble. Upon either side there ran canalised in the shining stone a little stream of perfectly clear water. From time to time they would pass a lovely shrine or statue which the country people had adorned with garlands. As they approached the city they discovered a noble bridge in the manner, my friend believed, of the Italian Renaissance, with strong elliptical arches and built, like all the rest of the way, of marble, while the balustrade upon either side of it was so disposed in short symmetrical columns as to be particularly grateful to the eye. Over this bridge there went to and fro a great concourse of people, all smiling, eager, happy and busy, largely acquainted, apparently, each with the others, nodding, exchanging news, and in a word forming a most blessed company.

As they entered the city my friend's companion, who had talked of many things upon their way and had seemed to unite the most perfect courtesy and modesty with the widest knowledge, asked him whether there was any food or drink to which he was particularly attached.

" For," said he, " I make a point whenever I entertain a guest—and that," he put in with a laugh, " is, I am glad to say, a thing that happens frequently—I make a point, I say, of asking him what he really prefers. It makes such a difference! "

My friend began his reply with those conventional phrases to which we are all accustomed, " That he would be only too happy to take whatever was set before him," " That the prospect of his hospitality was a sufficient guarantee of his satisfaction," and so forth: but his host would take no denial.

" No, no! " said he. " Do please say just what you prefer! It is so easy to arrange—if you only knew! . . . Come, I know the place better than you," he added, smiling again; " you have no conception of its resources. Pray tell me quite simply before we leave this street "— for they were now in a street of sumptuous and well-appointed shops—" exactly what shall be commissioned."

Moved by I know not what freedom of expression, and expansive in a degree which he had never yet known, my friend smiled back and said: " Well, to tell you the truth, some such meal as this would appeal to me: First two dozen green-bearded oysters of the Arcachon kind, opened upon the *deep* shell with all their juices preserved, and each exquisitely cleaned. These set upon pounded ice and served in that sort of dish which is contrived for *each* oyster to repose in its own little recess with a sort of side arrangement for the reception of the empty shells."

His host nodded gravely, as one who takes in all that is said to him.

" Next," said my friend, in an enthusiastic manner, " real and good Russian caviar, cold but not frozen, and so touched with lemon—

only just so touched—as to be perfect. With
this I think a little of the wine called Barsac
should be drunk, and that cooled to about thirty-
eight degrees—(Fahrenheit). After this a
True Bouillon, and by a True Bouillon," said
my friend with earnestness, " I mean a Bouillon
that has long simmered in the pot and has been
properly skimmed, and has been seasoned not
only with the customary herbs but also with a
suspicion of carrot and of onion, and a mere
breath of tarragon."

" Right!" said his host.   " Right!" nodding
with real appreciation.

" And next," said my friend, halting in the
street to continue his list, " I think there should
be eggs."

" Right," said his host once more approv-
ingly; " and shall we say——"

" No," interrupted my friend eagerly, " let
me speak. Eggs *sur-le-plat*, frizzled to the
exact degree."

" Just what I was about to suggest," answered his delighted entertainer, " and black

pepper, I hope, ground large upon them in fresh granules from a proper wooden mill."

" Yes! Yes!" said my friend, now lyric, " and with *sea* salt in large crystals."

On saying which both of them fell into a sort of ecstasy which my friend broke by adding:

" Something quite light to follow . . . preferably a sugar-cured Ham braised in white wine. Then, I think, spinach, not with the ham but after it; and that spinach cooked perfectly dry. We will conclude with some of the cheese called Brie. And for wine during all these latter courses we will drink the wine of Chinon: Chinon Grillé. What they call," he added slyly, " the *Fausse maigre;* for it is a wine thin at sight but full in the drinking of it."

" Good! Excellent!" said his host, clapping his hands together once with a gesture of finality. " And then after the lot you shall have coffee."

" Yes, coffee roasted during the meal and ground immediately before its concoction. And for liqueur . . ."

THE PLEASANT PLACE

My friend was suddenly taken with a little doubt. "I dare not ask," said he, "for the liqueur called Aquebus? Once only did I taste it. A monk gave it me on Christmas Eve four years ago and I think it is not known!"

"Oh, ask for it by all means!" said his host. "Why, we know it and love it in this place as though it were a member of the family!"

My friend could hardly believe his ears on hearing such things, and said nothing of cigars. But to his astonishment his host, putting his left hand on my friend's shoulder, looked him full in the face and said:

"And now shall *I* tell you about cigars?"

"I confess they were in my mind," said my friend.

"Why then," said his host with an expression of profound happiness, "there is a cigar in this town which is full of flavour, black in colour, which does not bite the tongue, and which none the less satisfies whatever tobacco does satisfy in man. When you smoke it you really dream."

"Why," said my friend humbly, "very well then, let us mention these cigars as the completion of our little feast."

"Little *feast*, indeed!" said his host, "why it is but a most humble meal. Anyhow, I am glad to have had from you a proper schedule of your pleasures of the table. In time to come when we know each other better, we will arrange other large and really satisfactory meals; but this will do very well for our initiatory lunch as it were." And he laughed merrily.

"But have I not given you great trouble?" said my friend.

"How little you will easily perceive," said his companion, "for in this town we have but to order and all is at once promptly and intelligently done." With that he turned into a small office where a commissary at once took down his order. "And now," said he emerging, "let us be home."

They went together down the turnings of a

couple of broad streets lined with great private palaces and public temples until they came to a garden which had no boundaries to it but which was open, and apparently the property of the city. But the people who wandered here were at once so few, so discreet and so courteous, my friend could not discover whether they were (as their salutes seemed to indicate) the dependents of his host, or merely acquaintances who recognized him upon their way.

This garden, as they proceeded, became more private and more domestic; it led by narrowing paths through high, diversified trees, until, beyond the screen of a great beech hedge, he saw the house . . . and it was all that a house should be!

Its clear, well set stone walls were in such perfect harmony with the climate and with the sky, its roof garden from which a child was greeting them upon their approach, so unexpected and so suitable, its arched open gallery was of so august a sort, and yet the domestic ornaments of its colonnade so familiar, that nothing could be conceived more appropriate for the residence of man.

The mere passage into this Home out of the warm morning daylight into the inner domestic cool, was a benediction, and in the courtyard which they thus entered a lazy fountain leaped and babbled to itself in a manner that filled the heart with ease.

" I do not know," said his host in a gentle whisper as they crossed the courtyard, " whether it is your custom to bathe before the morning meal or in the middle of the afternoon? "

" Why, sir," said my friend, " if I may tell the whole truth, I have no custom in the matter; but perhaps the middle of the afternoon would suit me best."

" By all means," said his host in a satisfied tone. " And I think you have chosen wisely, for the meal you have ordered will very shortly be prepared. But, for your refreshment at least, one of my friends shall put you in order, cool your hands and forehead, see to your face and hair, put comfortable sandals upon your feet and give you a change of raiment."

All of this was done. My friend's host did well to call the servant who attended upon his guest a " friend," for there was in this man's manner no trace of servility or of dependence, and yet an eager willingness for service coupled with a perfect reticence which was admirable to behold and feel.

When my friend had been thus refreshed he was conducted to a most exceptional little room. Four pictures were set in the walls of it, mosaics, they seemed—but he did not examine their medium closely. The room itself in its perfect lightness and harmony, with its view out through a large round arch upon the countryside beyond the walls (the old turrets of which made a framework for the view), exactly prepared him for the meal that was prepared.

While the oysters (delightful things!) were entering upon their tray and were being put upon the table, the host, taking my friend aside with an exquisite gesture of courteous privacy, led him through the window-arch on to a balcony without, and said, as they gazed upon the wall and the plain and the mouuntains beyond (and what a sight they were!) :

"There is one thing, my dear sir, that I should like to say to you before you eat . . . it is rather a delicate matter. . . . You will not mind my being perfectly frank?"

"Speak on, speak on," said my friend, who by this time would have confided any interests whatsoever into the hands of such a host.

"Well," said that host, continuing a little carefully, "it is this: as you can see we are very careful in this city to make men as happy as may be. We are happy ourselves, and we love to confer happiness upon others, strangers and travellers who honour us with their presence. But we find—I am very sorry to say we find . . . that is, we find from time to time that their *complete* happiness, no matter with what we may provide them, is dashed by certain forms of anxiety, the chief of which is anxiety with regard to their future receipts of money."

THE PLEASANT PLACE

My friend started.

" Nay," said his host hastily, " do not misunderstand me. I do not mean that preoccupations of business are alone so alarming. What I mean is that sometimes, yes, and I may say often (horrible as it seems to us!), our guests are in an active preoccupation about the petty business of finance. Some few have debts, it seems, in the wretched society from which they come, and of which, frankly, I know nothing. Others, though not indebted, feel insecure about the future. Others though wealthy .are oppressed by their responsibilities. Now," he continued firmly, " I must tell you once and for all that we have a custom here upon which we take no denial: *no denial whatsoever.* Every man who enters this city, who *honours* us by entering this city, is made free of *that* sort of nonsense, thank God! " And as he said this, my friend's host breathed a great sigh of relief. " It would be intolerable to us to think," he continued, " that our welcome and dear companions were suffering from such a tawdry thing as money-worry in our presence. So the matter is plainly this: whether you like it or whether you do not, the sum of £10,000 is already set down to your credit in the public bank of the city; whether you use it or not is your business; if you do not it is our custom to melt down an equivalent sum of gold and to cast it into the depths of the river, for we have of this metal an unfailing supply, and I confess we do not find it easy to understand the exaggerated value which other men place upon it."

"I do not know that I shall have occasion to use so magnificent a custom," said my friend with an extraordinary relief in his heart, "but I certainly thank you very kindly for its intention, and I shall not hesitate to use any sum that may be necessary for my continuing the great happiness which this city appears to afford."

"You have spoken well," said his host, seizing both his hands, "and your frankness compels me to another confession: We have at our disposal a means of discovering exactly how any one of our guests may stand: the responsibilities of the rich, the indebtedness of the embarrassed, the anxiety of those whose future may be precarious. May I tell you without discourtesy, that your own case is known to me and to two trustees, who are public officials—absolutely reliable—and whom, for that matter, you will not meet."

My friend must have looked incredulous, but his host continued firmly: " It is so, we have settled your whole matter, I am glad to say, on terms that settle all your liabilities and leave a further £50,000 to your credit in the public bank. But the size of the sum is in this city really of no importance. You may demand whatever you will, and enjoy, I hope, a complete security during your habitation here. And that habitation, both the Town Council and the National Government, beg you, through me, to extend to the whole of your life."

.   .   .   .   .

" Imagine," said my friend, " how I felt. . . . The oysters were now upon the table, and before them, ready for consumption, the caviar. The Barsac in its original bottle, cooled (need I say!) to exactly thirty-eight degrees, stood ready . . ."

At this point he stopped and gazed into the fire.

" But, my dear fellow," said I, " if you are coming to me for sympathy and simply succeed in making me hungry and cross . . ."

" No," said my friend with a sob, " you don't understand!" And he continued to gaze at the fire.

" Well, go *on*," said I angrily.

" There isn't any *on*," he said; " I woke!"

We both looked into the fire together for perhaps three minutes before I spoke and said:

" Will you have some wine? "

" No thank you," he answered sadly, " not *that* wine." Then he got up uneasily and moved for his umbrella and his galoshes, and the passage and the door. I thought he muttered, " You might have helped me."

THE PLEASANT PLACE

" How could I help you? " I said savagely.

" Well," he sighed, " I thought you could
. . . it was a bitter disappointment. Good
night! " And he went out again into the rain
and over the clay.

X

ON OMENS

ONLY the other day there was printed in a newspaper (what a lot of things they print in newspapers!) five lines which read thus:

"Calcutta, Thursday.

"An hour before the Viceroy left Calcutta on Wednesday for the last time lightning struck the flag over Government House, tearing it to shreds. This is considered to be an omen by the natives."

The Devil they did! A superstitious chap, your native, and we have outgrown such things. But it is really astonishing when you come to think of it how absurdly credulous the human race has been for thousands of years about omens, and still is—everywhere except here. And by the way, what a curious thing it is that

only in one country, and only in one little tiny
circle of it should this terrible vice have been
eradicated from the human mind! If one were
capable of paradox one would say that the
blessing conferred upon us few enlightened people in England was providential; but that would
be worse superstition than the other. There
seems to be a tangle somewhere. Anyhow, there
it is: people have gone on by the million and
for centuries and centuries believing in omens.
It is an illusion. It is due to a frame of mind.
That which the enlightened person easily dis-
covers to be a coincidence, the Native, that is,
the person living in a place, thinks to be in some
way due to a Superior Power. It is a way Natives have. Nothing warps the mind like being a Native.

The Reform Bill passed in 1832 and destroyed not only the Pot-Wallopers, but also
the ancient Constitution of the country. From
that time onwards we have been free. When
the thing was thoroughly settled (and the
old Poor Law was being got rid of into the

bargain), the old House of Lords, and the old House of Commons, they caught fire, " and they did get burnt down to the ground." Those are the very words of an old man who saw it happen and who told me about it. The misfortune was due to the old tallies of the Exchequer catching fire, and this silly old man, who saw it happen (he was a child of six at the time), has always thought it was an Omen. It has been explained to him, not only by good, kind ladies who go and visit him and see that he gets no money or beer, but also from the Pulpit of St. Margaret's Church, Westminster (where he regularly attends Divine Service by kind permission of the Middle Class, and in the vain hope of cadging alms), that there is no such thing as Providence, and that if he lets his mind dwell on Omens he will end by believing in God. But the old man is much too old to receive a new idea, so he goes on believing that the burning of old St. Stephen's was an Omen.

Not so the commercial traveller, who told me in an hotel the other day the story of the market-woman of Devizes, to exemplify the gross superstitions of our fathers.

It seems that the market-woman, sometime when George III was King, had taken change of a sovereign on market-day, from a purchaser, when there were no witnesses, and then, in the presence of witnesses, demanded the change again. The man most solemnly affirmed that he had paid her, to which she replied: " If I have taken your money may God strike me dead." The moment these words were out of the market-woman's lips, an enormous great jagged, forked, fiery dart of lightning, three miles long, leapt out of a distant cloud, and shrivelled her up. " Whereupon," ended the commercial traveller, " the people of Devizes *in those days* were so superstitious that they thought it was a judgment, they did! And they put up a plate in commemoration. Such foolishness!" It is sad to think of the people of Devizes and their darkness of understanding when George III was King. But, upon the other hand, it is a joy to think of the fresh,

clear minds of the people of Devizes to-day.
For though, every Sunday morning, about half
an hour after Church time, every single man
and woman who had shirked Church, Chapel,
Mosque or Synagogue, each according to his
or her creed should fall down dead of no apparent illness, and though upon the forehead
of each one so taken, the survivors returning
from their services, meetings or what-not,
should find clearly written in a vivid blue the
Letters of Doom. None the less the people of
Devizes would, it is to be hoped, retain their
mental balance, and distinguish between a coincidence (which is the only true explanation of
such things) and fond imaginings of super-
natural possibilities.

There is an old story and a good one to
teach us how to fight against any weakness of
the sort, which is this. Two old gentlemen
who had never met before were in a first-class
railway carriage of a train that does not stop
until it gets to Bristol. They were talking
about ghosts. One of them was a parson,

the other was a layman. The layman said he did not believe in ghosts. The parson was very much annoyed, tried to convince him, and at last said, "After all, you'd have to believe in one if you saw one."

"No, I shouldn't," said the layman sturdily. "I should know it was an illusion."

Then the old parson got very angry indeed, and said in a voice shaking with self-restraint:

"Well, you've got to believe in ghosts now, for I am one!" Whereat he immediately vanished into the air.

The old layman, finding himself well rid of a bad business, shook himself together, wrapped his rug round his knees, and began to read his paper, for he knew very well that it was an illusion.

Of the same sturdy sense was Isaac Newton, when a lady came to him who had heard he was an astrologer, and asked him where she had dropped her purse, somewhere between Shooter's Hill and London Bridge. She would not believe that the Baronet (or knight, I forget which) could be ignorant of such things, and she came about fourteen times. So to be rid of her Newton, on the occasion of her last visit, put on an old flowered dressing-gown, and made himself a conical paper hat, and put on great blue goggles, and drew a circle on the floor, and said " Abracadabra!" " The front of Greenwich Hospital, the third great window from the southern end. On the grass just beneath it I see a short devil crouched upon a purse of gold." Off went the female, and sure enough under that window she found her purse. Whereat, instead of hearing the explanation (there was none) she thought it was an Omen.

Remember this parable. It is enormously illuminating.

XI

THE BOOK

THIS is written to dissuade all rich men from queering the pitch of us poor litteratoors, who have to write or starve. It is about a Mr. Foley: a Mr. Charles Foley, a banker and the son of a banker, who in middle life, that is at forty, saw no more use in coming to his office every day, but began to lead the life of a man of leisure. Next, being exceedingly rich he was prompted, of course, to write a book. The thing that prompted him to write a book was a thought, an idea. It took him suddenly as ideas will, one Saturday evening as he was walking home from his Club. It was a fine night and the idea seemed to come upon him out of the sky. This was the idea: that men produce such and such art in architecture and society and so forth, on account of the kind of climate they live in. Such a thought had never come to him before and very probably to no other man. It was simple like a seed—and yet, as he turned it over, what enormous possibilities.

He lay awake half the night examining it. It spread out like a great tree and explained every human thing on earth; at least if to climate one added one or two other things, such as height above the sea and consequent rarity of the air and so forth—but perhaps all these could be included in climate.

Hitherto every one had imagined that nations and civilisations had each their temperament and tendency or genius, but those words were only ways of saying that one did not know what it was. *He* knew: Charles Foley did. He had caught the inspiration suddenly as it passed. He slept the few last hours of the night in a profound repose, and next day he was at it. He was writing that book.

He was a business-man—luckily for him. He did not speak of the great task until it was done. He was in no need of money—luckily for him. He could afford to wait until the last pages had satisfied him. Life had taught him that one could do nothing in business unless one had something in one's hands. He would come to the publisher with something in his hands, to wit, with this MSS. He had no doubt about the title. He would call it " MAN AND NATURE." The title had come to him in a sort of flash after the idea. Anyhow, that was the title, and he felt it to be a very part of his being.

He had fixed upon his publisher. He rang him up to make an appointment. The publisher received him with charming courtesy. It was the publisher himself who received him; not the manager, nor the secretary, nor any one like that, but the real person, the one who had the overdraft at the Bank.

He treated Mr. Charles Foley so well that Mr. Foley tasted a new joy which was the joy of sincere praise received. He was in the liberal arts now. He had come into a second world. His mere wealth had never given him this. When the publisher had heard what Mr. Charles Foley had to say, he scratched the tip of his nose with his forefinger, and suggested that Mr. Foley should pay for the printing and the binding of the book, and that then the publisher should advertise it and sell it, and give Mr. Foley so much.

But Mr. Foley would have none of this. He was a business man and he could see through a brick wall as well as any one. So the publisher made this suggestion and that suggestion and talked all round about it. He was evidently keen to have the book. Mr. Foley could see that. At last the publisher made what Mr. Foley thought for the first time a sound business proposition, which was that he should publish the book in the ordinary way and then that he and Mr. Foley should share and share alike. If there was a loss they would divide it, but if there was a profit they would divide that. Mr. Foley was glad that he came to a sensible business decision at last, and closed with him. The date of publication also was agreed upon: it was to be the 15th of April. " In order," said the publisher, "that we may catch the London season." Mr. Charles Foley suggested August, but the publisher assured him that August was a rotten time for books.

Only the very next day Mr. Foley entered upon the responsibilities which are inseparable from the joys of an author. He received a letter from the publisher, saying that it seemed that another book had been written under the title "Man and Nature," that he dared not publish under that title lest the publishers of the other volume should apply for an injunction.

Mr. Foley suffered acutely. He left his breakfast half finished; ran into town in his motor, as agonized in every block of the traffic as though he had to catch a train; was kept waiting half an hour in the publisher's office because the principal had not yet arrived, and, when he did arrive, was persuaded that there was nothing to be done. The Courts wouldn't allow "Man and Nature," the publisher was sure of that. He kept on shaking his great big silly head until it got on Mr. Foley's nerves. But there was no way out of it, so Mr. Foley changed the title to " ART AND ENVIRONMENT " —it was the publisher's secretary who suggested this new title.

He got home to luncheon, to which he now remembered he had asked a friend—a man who played golf. Mr. Foley did not want to make a fool of himself, so he led up very cautiously at luncheon to his great question, which was this: " How does the title ' Art and Environment ' sound? " He had a friend, he said, who wanted to know. On hearing this Mr. Foley's golfing friend gave a loud guffaw, and said it *sounded* all right; so did the *Origin of Species*. It would come out about the same time, and then he spent three or four minutes trying to remember who the old johnny was who wrote it, but Mr. Foley was already at the telephone in the hall. He was not happy; he had rung up the publisher. The publisher was at luncheon. Mr. Foley damned the publisher. Could he speak to the manager? To the sec-

retary? To one of the clerks? To the little
dog? In his anger he was pleased to be
facetious. He heard the manager's voice:

" Yes, is that Mr. Foley? "

" Yes, about that title."

" Oh, yes, I thought you'ld ring up. It's
impossible, you know, it's been used before;
and there's no doubt at all that the University
printers would apply for an injunction."

" Well, I can't wait," shouted Mr. Foley into
the receiver.

" You can't what? " said the manager. " I
can't hear you, you are talking too loud."

" I can't wait," said Mr. Foley in a lower
tone and strenuously. " Suggest something
quick."

The manager could be heard thinking at the
end of the live wire. At last he said, " Oh, anything." Mr. Foley used a horrible word and
put back the receiver.

He went back to his golfing friend who was
drinking some port steadily with cheese, and
said: " Look here, that friend of mine I have

just been telephoning to says he wants another title."

" What for? " said the golfing friend, his mouth full of cheese.

" Oh, for his book of course," said Mr. Foley sharply.

" Sorry, I thought it was politics," answered his friend, his mouth rather less full. Then a bright thought struck him.

" What's the book about? "

" Well, it's about art and . . . climate, you know."

" Why, then," said the friend stolidly, " why not call it ' Art and Climate '? "

" That's a good idea," said Mr. Foley, stroking his chin.

He hurried indecently, turned the poor golfing friend out, hurried up to town in his motor in order to make them call the book " Art and Climate." When he got there he found the real publisher, who hummed and hawed and said: " All this changing of titles will be very expensive, you know." Mr. Foley could not help that, it had to be done, so the book was called " Art and Climate," and then it was printed, and seventy copies were sent out to the Press and it was reviewed by three papers.

One of the papers said:

" Mr. Charles Foley has written an interesting essay upon the effect of climate upon art, upon such conditions as will affect it whether adversely or the contrary. The point of view is an original one and gives food for thought."

Mr. Foley thought this notice quite too short and imperfect.

The second paper had a column about it, nearly all of which was made out of bits cut right out of the book, but without acknowledgment or in inverted commas. In between the bits cut out there were phrases like, " Are we however to believe that . . ." and " Some in this connection would decide that. . . ." But all the rest were bits cut out of his book.

THE BOOK

The third review was in *The Times*, and in very small type between brackets. All it did was to give a list of the chapters and a sentence out of the preface.

Mr. Foley sold thirty copies of his book, gave away seventy-four and lent two. The publisher assured him that books like that did not have a large immediate sale as a novel did; they had a slow, steady sale.

It was about the middle of May that the publisher assured him of this. In June the solicitors of a Professor at Yale acting for the learned man in this country, threatened an action concerning a passage in the book which was based entirely upon the Professor's copyright work. Mr. Foley admitted his high indebtedness to the Professor, and wore a troubled look for days. He had always thought it quite legitimate in the world of art to use another person's work if one acknowledged it. At last the thing was settled out of court for quite a small sum, £150 or £200, or something like that.

Then everything was quiet and the sales went very slowly. He only sold a half-dozen all the rest of the summer.

In the autumn the publisher wrote him a note asking whether he might act upon Clause 15 of the contract. Mr. Foley was a business man. He looked up the contract and there he saw these words:

"If after due time has elapsed in the opinion of the publisher, a book shall not be warrantable at its existing price, change of price shall be made in it at the discretion of the publisher or of the author, or both, or each, subject to the conditions of Clause 9."

Turning to Clause 9, Mr. Foley discovered the words:

"All questions of price, advertisements, binding, paper, printing, etc., shall be vested in Messrs. Towkem Bingo and Platt, hereinafter called the Publishers."

99

THE BOOK

He puzzled a great deal about these two clauses, and at last he thought, " Oh, well, they know more than I do about it," so he just telegraphed back, " Yes."

On the first of the New Year Mr. Foley got a most astonishing document. It was a printed sheet with a lot of lines written in red ink and an account. On the one side there was " By sales £18," then there was a long red line drawn down like a Z, and at the bottom, " £241 17s. 4½d.," and in front of this the word " Balance," then the two were added together and made £259 17s. 4½d. Under this sum there were two lines drawn.

On the other side of the document there was a whole regiment of items, one treading upon another's heels. There was paper, and printing, and corrections, binding, warehousing, storage, cataloguing, advertising, travelling, circularizing, packing, and what I may call with due respect to the reader, " the devil and all." The whole of which added up to no less than the monstrous sum of £519 14s. 9d. Under this was written in small letters in red ink, " Less 50% as per agreement," and then at the bottom that nasty figure, " £259 17s. 4½d.," and there was a little request in a round hand that the balance of £241 17s. 4½d. should be paid at Mr. Foley's convenience.

Mr. Foley, white with rage, acted as a business man always should. He wrote a short note refusing to pay a penny, and demanding the rest of the unsold copies. He got a lengthier and stronger note from Messrs. Towkem and Thingummebob, referring to his letter, to Clause 9 and to Clause 15, informing him that the remainder of the stock had been sold at a penny each to a firm of papermakers in the North of England, and respectfully pressing for immediate payment.

Mr. Foley put the matter in the hands of his solicitors and they ran him up a bill for £37 odd, but it was well worth it because they persuaded him not to go into court, so in the long run he had to pay no more than £278 17s. 4½d., unless you count the postage and the travelling.

THE BOOK

Now you know what happened to Mr. Foley and his book, and what will happen to *you* if you are a rich man and poach on my preserves.

XII

THE SERVANTS OF THE RICH

Do you mark there, down in the lowest point and innermost funnel of Hell Fire Pit, souls writhing in smoke, themselves like glowing smoke and tortured in the flame? You ask me what they are. These are the Servants of the Rich: the men who in their mortal life opened the doors of the Great Houses and drove the carriages and sneered at the unhappy guests.

Those larger souls that bear the greatest doom and manifest the more dreadful suffering, they are the Butlers boiling in molten gold.

"What!" you cry, "is there then, indeed, as I once heard in childhood, justice for men and an equal balance, and a final doom for evil deeds?" There is! Look down into the murky hollow and revere the awful accomplishment of human things.

THE SERVANTS OF THE RICH

These are the men who would stand with powder on their heads like clowns, dressed in fantastic suits of gold and plush, with an ugly scorn upon their faces, and whose pleasure it was (while yet their time of probation lasted) to forget every human bond and to cast down the nobler things in man: treating the artist as dirt and the poet as a clown; and beautiful women, if they were governesses or poor relations or in any way dependents, as a meet object for silent mockery. But now their time is over and they have reaped the harvest which they sowed. Look and take comfort, all you who may have suffered at their hands.

Come closer. See how each separate sort suffers its peculiar penalty. There go a hopeless shoal through the reek: their doom is an eternal sleeplessness and a nakedness in the gloom. There is nothing to comfort them, not even memory: and they know that for ever and for ever they must plunge and swirl, driven before the blasts, now hot, now icy, of their everlasting pain. These are those men who were wont to come into the room of the Poor Guest at early morning with a steadfast and assured step and a look of insult. These are those who would take the tattered garments and hold them at arm's length as much as to say: " What rags these scribblers wear! " and then, casting them over the arm with a gesture that meant: " Well, they must be brushed, but Heaven knows if they will stand it without coming to pieces! " would next discover in the pockets a great quantity of middle-class things, and notably loose tobacco.

These are they that would then take out with the utmost patience, private letters, money, pocket-books, knives, dirty crumpled stamps, scraps of newspapers, broken cigarettes, pawn tickets, keys, and much else, muttering within themselves so that one could almost hear it with their lips: " What a jumble these paupers stuff their shoddy with! They do not even know that in the Houses of the Great it is not customary to fill the pockets! They do not know that the

Great remove at night from their pockets such few trinkets of diamonded gold as they may contain. Where were they born or bred? To think that *I* should have to serve such cattle! No matter! He has brought money with him I am glad to see—borrowed, no doubt—and I will bleed him well."

Such thoughts one almost heard as one lay in the Beds of the Great despairing. Then one would see him turn one's socks inside out, which is a ritual with the horrid tribe. Then a great bath would be trundled in and he would set beside it a great can and silently pronounce the judgment that whatever else was forgiven the middle-class one thing would not be forgiven them—the neglect of the bath, of the splashing about of the water and of the adequate wetting of the towel.

All these things we have suffered, you and I, at their hands. But be comforted. They writhe in Hell with their fellows.

That man who looked us up and down so insolently when the great doors were opened in

St. James' Square and who thought one's boots so comic. He too, and all his like, burn separately. So does that fellow with the wine that poured it out ungenerously, and clearly thought that we were in luck's way to get the bubbly stuff at all in any measure. He that conveyed his master's messages with a pomp that was instinct with scorn and he that drove you to the station, hardly deigning to reply to your timid sentences and knowing well your tremors and your abject ill-ease. Be comforted. He too burns.

It is the custom in Hell when this last batch of scoundrels, the horsey ones, come up in batches to be dealt with by the authorities thereof, for them first to be asked in awful tones how many pieces of silver they have taken from men below the rank of a squire, or whose income was less than a thousand pounds a year, and the truth on this they are compelled by Fate to declare, whereupon, before their tortures begin, they receive as many stripes as they took florins: nor is there any defect in the arrangement of divine justice in their regard, save that the money is not refunded to us.

Cooks, housemaids, poor little scullery-maids, under-gardeners, estate carpenters of all kinds, small stable lads, and in general all those humble Servants of the Rich who are debarred by their insolent superiors from approaching the guests and neither wound them with contemptuous looks, nor follow these up by brigandish demands for money, *these* you will not see in this Pit of Fire. For them is reserved a high place in Paradise, only a little lower than that supreme and cloudy height of bliss wherein repose the happy souls of all who on this earth have been Journalists.

But Game-Keepers, more particularly those who make a distinction and will take nothing less than gold (nay *Paper!*), and Grooms of the Chamber, and all such, these suffer torments for ever and for ever. So has Immutable Justice decreed and thus is the offended majesty of man avenged.

And what, you will ask me perhaps at last,

what of the dear old family servants, who are *so* good, *so* kind, *so* attached to Master Arthur and to Lady Jane?

Ah! . . . Of these the infernal plight is such that I dare not set it down!

There is a special secret room in Hell where their villainous hypocrisy and that accursed mixture of yielding and of false independence wherewith they flattered and be-fooled their masters; their thefts, their bullying of beggar-men, have at last a full reward. Their eyes are no longer sly and cautious, lit with the pretence of affection, nor are they here rewarded with good fires and an excess of food, and perquisites and pensions. But they sit hearthless, jibbering with cold, and they stare broken at the prospect of a dark Eternity. And now and then one or another, an aged serving-man or a white-haired housekeeper, will wring their hands and say: " Oh, that I had once, only once, shown in my mortal life some momentary gleam of honour, independence, or dignity! Oh, that I had but once stood up in my freedom and spoken to the Rich as I should! Then it would have been remembered for me and I should now have been spared this place—but it is too late!"

For there is no repentance known among the Servants of the Rich, nor any exception to their vileness; they are hated by men when they live, and when they die they must for all eternity consort with demons.

XIII

THE JOKE

THERE are two kinds of jokes, those jokes that are funny because they are true, and those jokes that would be funny anyhow. Think it out and you will find that that is a great truth. Now the joke I have here for the delectation of the broken-hearted is of the first sort. It is funny because it is true. It is about a man whom I really saw and really knew and touched, and on occasions treated ill. He was. The sunlight played upon his form. Perhaps he may still flounder under the light of the sun, and not yet have gone down into that kingdom whose kings are less happy than the poorest hind upon the upper fields.

It was at College that I knew him and I retained my acquaintance with him—Oh, I retained it in a loving and cherishing manner—until he was grown to young manhood. I would keep it still did Fate permit me so to do, for he was a treasure. I have never met anything so complete for the purposes of laughter, though I am told there are many such in the society which bred his oafish form.

He was a noble in his own country, which was somewhere in the pine-forests of the Germanies, and his views of social rank were far, far too simple for the silent subtlety of the English Rich. In his poor turnip of a mind he ordered all men thus:

First, reigning sovereigns and their families.

Secondly, mediatized people.

Third, Princes.

Fourth, Dukes.

Fifth, Nobles.

Then came a little gap, and after that little gap The Others.

Most of us in our College were The Others. But he, as I have said, was a noble in his distant land.

He had not long been among the young Englishmen when he discovered that a difficult tangle of titles ran hither and thither among them like random briars through an undergrowth. There were Honourables, and there were Lords, and Heaven knows what, and there were two Sirs, and altogether it puzzled him.

He couldn't understand why a man should be called Mr. Jinks, and his brother Lord Blefauscu, and then if a man could be called Lord Blefauscu while his father Lord Brobdignag was alive, how was it that quite a Fresher should be called Sir Howkey—no—he was Sir John Howkey: and when the Devil did one put in the Christian name and when didn't one, and why should one, and what was the order of precedence among all these?

I think that last point puzzled him more than the rest, for in his own far distant land in the pine-woods, where peasants uglier than sin grovelled over the potato crop and called him " Baron," there were no such devilish contraptions, but black was black and white was white. Here in this hypocritical England, to which his father had sent him as an exile, everything was so wrapped up in deceiving masks! There was the Captain of the Eleven, or the President of the Boat Club. By the time he had mastered that there might be great men not only without the actual title (he had long ago despaired of that), but without so much as cousinship to one, he would stumble upon a fellow with nothing whatsoever to distinguish him, not even the High Jump, and yet " in " with the highest. It tortured him I can tell you! After he had sat upon several Fourth Year men (he himself a Fresher), from an error as to their rank, after he had been duly thrown into the water, blackened as to his face with blacking, sentenced to death in a court-martial and duly shot with a blank cartridge (an unpleasant thing by the way looking down a barrel) ; after he had had his boots, of which there were seven pair, packed with earth, and in each one a large geranium planted; after all these things had happened to him in his pursuit of an Anglo-German understanding, he approached a lanky, pot-bellied youth whom he had discovered with certitude to be the cousin of a Duke, and begged him secretly to befriend him in a certain matter, which was this:

The Baron out of the Germanies proposed to give a dinner to no less than thirty people and he begged the pot-bellied youth in all secrecy to collect for him an assembly worthy of his rank and to give him privately not only their names but their actual precedence according to which he would arrange them at the table upon his right and upon his left.

But what did the pot-bellied youth do? Why he went out and finding all his friends one after the other he said:

" You know Sausage? "

" Yes," said they, for all the University knew Sausage.

" Well, he is going to give a dinner," said the pot-bellied one, who was also slow of speech, " and you have to come, but I'm going to say you are the Duke of Rochester " (or whatever title he might have chosen). And so speaking, and so giving the date and place he

115

would go on to the next. Then, when he had collected not thirty but sixty of all his friends and acquaintances, he sought out the noble Teuton again and told him that he could not possibly ask only thirty men without lifelong jealousies and hatreds, so sixty were coming, and the Teuton with some hesitation (for he was fond of money) agreed.

Never shall I forget the day when those sixty were ushered solemnly into a large Reception Room in the Hotel, blameless youths of varying aspect, most of them quite sober—since it was but 7 o'clock—presented one by one to the host of the evening, each with his title and style.

To those whom he recognized as equals the Aristocrat spoke with charming simplicity. Those who were somewhat his inferiors (the lords by courtesy and the simple baronets) he put immediately at their ease; and even the Honourables saw at a glance that he was a man of the world, for he said a few kind words to each. As for a man with no handle to his name, there was not one of the sixty so low, except a Mr. Poopsibah of whom the gatherer of that feast whispered to the host that he could not but ask him because, though only a second cousin, he was the heir to the Marquis of Quirk —hence his Norman name.

It was a bewilderment to the Baron, for he might have to meet the man later in life as the Marquis of Quirk, whereas for the moment he was only Mr. Poopsibah, but anyhow he was put at the bottom of the table—and that was how the trouble began.

In my time—I am talking of the nineties— young men drank wine: it was before the Bishop of London had noted the Great Change. And Mr. Poopsibah and his neighbour—Lord Henry Job—were quite early in the Feast occupied in a playful contest which ended in Mr. Poop- sibah's losing his end seat and going to grass. He rose, not unruffled, with a burst collar, and glared a little uncertainly over the assembled wealth and lineage of the evening. Lord Benin (the son of our great General Lord Ashantee of Benin—his real name was Mitcham, God Rest His Soul) addressed to the unreal Poopsibah an epithet then fashionable, now almost forgotten, but always unprintable. Mr. Poopsibah, forgetting what nobility imposes, immediately hurled at him an as yet half-emptied bottle of Champagne.

Then it was that the bewildered Baron learnt for the last time—and for that matter for the first time—to what the Island Race can rise when it really lets itself go.

I remember (I was a nephew if I remember right) above the din and confusion of light (for candles also were thrown) loud appeals as in a tone of command, and then as in a tone of supplication, both in the unmistakable accents of the Cousins overseas, and I even remember what I may call the Great Sacrilege of that evening when Lord Gogmagog seizing our host affectionately round the neck, and pressing the back of his head with his large and red left hand, attempted to grind his face into the tablecloth, after a fashion wholly unknown to the haughty lords of the Teufel-wald.

During the march homewards—an adventure enlightened with a sharp skirmish and two losses at the hands of the police—I know not what passed through the mind of the youth who had hitherto kept so careful a distinction between blood and blood: whether like Hannibal he swore eternal hatred to the English, or whether in his patient German mind he noted it all down as a piece of historical evidence to be used in his diplomatic career, we shall not be told. I think in the main he was simply bewildered: bewildered to madness.

Of the many other things we made him do before Eights Week I have no space to tell: How he asked us what was the fashionable sport and how we told him Polo and made him buy a Polo pony sixteen hands high, with huge great bones and a broken nose, explaining to him that it was stamina and not appearance that the bluff Englishman loved in a horse. How we made him wear his arms embroidered upon his handkerchief (producing several for a pattern and taking the thing as a commonplace by sly allusion for many preparatory days). How we told him that it was the custom to call every Sunday afternon for half an hour upon the wife of every married Don of one's College: How we challenged him to the Great College feat of throwing himself into the river at midnight: How finally we persuaded him that the ancient custom of the University demanded the presentation to one's Tutor at the end of term of an elaborate thesis one hundred pages long upon some subject of Theology: How he was carefully warned that surprise was the essence of this charming tradition and not a word of it must be breathed to the august recipient of the favour: How he sucked in the knowledge that the more curious and strange the matter the higher would be his place in the schools, and how the poor fool elaborately wasted what God gives such men for brains in the construction of a damning refutation against the Monophysites: How his tutor, a humble little nervous fool, thought he was having his leg pulled—all these things I have no space to tell you now.

But he was rich! Doubtless by the custom of his country he is now in some great position plotting the ruin of Britannia and certainly she deserves it in his case. He was most unmercifully ragged.

XIV

THE SPY

ONE day as I was walking along the beach at Southsea, I saw a little man sitting upon a camp-stool and very carefully drawing the Old Round Stone Fort which stands in the middle of the shallow water, one of the four that so stand, and which looks from Southsea as though it were about half-way across to the Island.

I said to him: " Sir, why are you drawing that old Fort? "

He answered: " I am a German Spy, and the reason I draw that Fort is to provide information for my Government which may be useful to it in case of war with this country."

When the gentleman sitting upon the camp-stool, who was drawing the Old Round Stone Fort in the middle of the water, talked like this he annoyed me very much.

" You merely waste your time," said I.

"These Forts were put up nearly sixty years ago, and they are quite useless."

"I know nothing about that," said the little man—he had hair like hemp and prominent weak blue eyes of a glazed sort, and altogether he struck me as a fool of no insignificant calibre —"I know nothing about that. I obey orders. I was told to draw this Fort, and that I am now doing."

"You do not draw well," said I, "but that is neither here nor there. I mean that what you draw is not beautiful. What I really want to know is why in thunder you were told to draw that round stone barrel, for which no one in Europe would give a five-pound note."

"I have nothing to do with all that," said the little man again, still industriously drawing. "I was told to draw that Fort, and that Fort I draw." And he went on drawing the Old Round Stone Fort.

"Can you not tell me for whom you are drawing it?" said I at last.

"Yes," said he, "with great pleasure. I am

drawing it for his King-like and Kaiser-like Majesty By the Grace of God and the Authority of the Holy See, William, King of Prussia, Margrave of Brandenburg, Duke of Romshall, Count Hohenzollern and of the Great German Empire, Emperor."

With that he went on drawing the Old Round Stone Fort.

"I do assure you most solemnly," said I again, "that you can be of no use whatever to your master in this matter. There are no guns upon that ridiculous thing; it has even been turned into a hotel."

But the little man paid no attention to what I said. He went on obeying orders. He had often heard that this was the strength of his race.

"How could there conceivably be any guns on it?" said I imploringly. "Do think what you are at! Do look at the range between you and Ryde! Do consider what modern gunnery is! Do wake up, do!"

But the little man with hair like hemp said

again: "I know nothing about all that. I am a lieutenant in the High Spy Corps, and I have been told to draw this Fort and I must draw it." And he went on drawing the Old Round Stone Fort.

Then gloom settled upon my spirit, for I thought that civilization was in peril if men such as he really existed and really went on in this fashion.

However, I went back into Southsea, into the town, and there I bought a chart. Then I struck off ranges upon the chart and marked them in pencil, and I also marked the Fairway through Spithead into Portsmouth Harbour. Then I came back to the little man, and I said: "Do look at this!"

He looked at it very patiently and carefully, but at the end of so looking at it he said: "I do not understand these things. I do not belong to the High Map-making Corps; I belong to the Spy Corps, and I have orders to draw this Fort." And he went on drawing the Old Round Stone Fort.

Then, seeing I could not persuade him, I went into a neighbouring church which is dedicated to the Patron of Spies, to wit, St. Judas, and I prayed for this man. I prayed thus:

" Oh, St. Judas! Soften the flinty heart of this Spy, and turn him, by your powerful intercession, from his present perfectly useless occupation of drawing the Old Round Stone Fort to something a little more worthy of his distinguished mission and the gallant profession he adorns."

When I had prayed thus diligently for half an hour something within me told me that it was useless, and when I got back to the seashore I found out what the trouble was. Prayers went off my little man like water off a cabbageleaf. My little man with hair like hemp was a No-Goddite, for he so explained to me in a conversation we had upon the Four Last Things.

" I have done my drawing," he said at the end of this conversation (and he said it in a tone of great satisfaction). " Now I shall go back to Germany."

"No," said I, "you shall do nothing of the kind. I will have you tried first in a court, and you shall be sent to prison for being a Spy."

"Very well," said he, and he came with me to the court.

The Magistrate tried him, and did what they call in the newspapers "looking very grave," that is, he looked silly and worried. At last he determined not to put the Spy in prison because there was not sufficient proof that he was a Spy.

"Although," he added, "I have little doubt but that you have been prying into the most important military secrets of the country."

After that I took the Spy out of court again and gave him some dinner, and that night he went back home to Germany with his drawing of the Old Round Stone Fort.

It is certainly an extraordinary way of doing business, but that is their look-out. *They* think they are efficient, and *we* think they are efficient, and when two people of opposite interests are agreed on such a matter it is not for third parties to complain.

XV

THE YOUNG PEOPLE

ONE of my amusements, a mournful one I admit, upon these fine spring days, is to watch in the streets of London the young people, and to wonder if they are what I was at their age.

There is an element in human life which the philosophers have neglected, and which I am at a loss to entitle, for I think no name has been coined for it. But I am not at a loss to describe it. It is that change in the proportion of things which is much more than a mere change in perspective, or in point of view. It is that change which makes Death so recognisable and too near; achievement necessarily imperfect, and desire necessarily mixed with calculation. It is more than that. It is a sort of seeing things from that far side of them, which was only guessed at or heard of at second hand in earlier years, but which is now palpable and part of the senses: known. All who have passed a certain age know what I mean.

This change, not so much in the aspect of things as in the texture of judgment, may mislead one when one judges youth; and it is best to trust to one's own memory of one's own youth if one would judge the young.

There I see a boy of twenty-five looking solemn enough, and walking a little too stiffly down Cockspur Street. Does he think himself immortal, I wonder, as I did? Does the thought of oblivion appal him as it did me? That he continually suffers in his dignity, that he thinks the passers-by all watch him, and that he is in terror of any singularity in dress or gesture, I can well believe, for that is common to all youth. But does he also, as did I and those of my time, purpose great things which are quite unattainable, and think the summit of success in any art to be the natural wage of living?

Then other things occur to me. Do these young people suffer or enjoy all our old illu-

sions? Do they think the country invincible?
Do they vaguely distinguish mankind into rich
and poor, and think that the former from whom
they spring are provided with their well-being
by some natural and fatal process, like the re-
currence of day and night? Are they as full
of the old taboos of what a gentleman may and
may not do? I wonder!—Possibly they are. I
have not seen one of them wearing a billycock
hat with a tail coat, nor one of them smoking a
pipe in the street. And is life divided for them
to-day as it was then, into three periods: their
childhood; their much more important years
at a public school (which last fill up most of
their consciousness); their new untried occupation?

And do they still so grievously and so happily
misjudge mankind? I think they must, judging by their eyes. I think they too believe that
industry earns an increasing reward, that what
is best done in any trade is best recognised
and best paid; that labour is a happy business;
and that women are of two kinds: the young

who go about to please them, the old to whom they are indifferent.

Do they drink? I suppose so. They do not show it yet. Do they gamble? I conceive they do. Are their nerves still sound? Of that there can be no doubt! See them hop on and off the motor 'buses and cross the streets!

And what of their attitude towards the labels? Do they take, as I did, every man much talked of for a great man? Are they diffident when they meet such men? And do they feel themselves to be in the presence of gods? I should much like to put myself into the mind of one of them and to see if, to that generation the simplest of all social lies is Gospel. If it is so, I must suppose they think a Prime Minister, a Versifier, an Ambassador, a Lawyer who frequently comes up in the Press, to be some very superhuman person. And doubtless also they ascribe a sort of general quality to all much-talked-of or much-be-printed men, putting them on one little shelf apart, and all the rest of England in a ruck below.

THE YOUNG PEOPLE

Then this thought comes to me. What of their bewilderment? We used all to be so bewildered! Things did not fit in with the very simple and rigid scheme that was our most undoubted creed of the State. The motives of most commercial actions seemed inscrutable save to a few base contemporaries no older than ourselves, but cads, men who would always remain what we had first known them to be, small clerks upon the make. At what age, I wonder, to this generation will come the discovery that of *these* men and of *such* material the Great are made; and will the long business of discovery come to sadden them as late as it came to their elders?

I must believe that young man walking down Cockspur Street thinks that all great poets, all great painters, all great writers, all great statesmen, are those of whom he reads, and are all possessed of unlimited means and command the world. Further, I must believe that the young man walking down Cockspur Street (he has got to Northumberland Avenue by now), lives in a static world. For him things are immovable. There are the old: fathers and mothers and uncles; the very old are there, grandfathers, nurses, provosts, survivors. Only in books does one find at that age the change of human affection, child-bearing, anxiety for money, and death. All the children (he thinks) will be always children, and all the lovely women always young. And loyalty and generous regards are twin easy matters reposing natively in the soul, and as yet unbetrayed.

Well, if they are all like that, or even most of them, the young people, quite half the world is happy. Not one of that happy half remembers the Lion of Northumberland House, or the little streets there were behind the Foreign Office, or the old Strand, or Temple Bar, or what Coutts's used to be like, or Simpson's, or Soho as yet uninvaded by the great and good Lord Shaftesbury. No one of the young can pleasantly recall the Metropolitan Board of Works.

And for them, all the new things—houses

which are veils of mud on stilts of iron, advertisements that shock the night, the rush of taxi-cabs and the Yankee hotels—are the things that always were and always will be.

A year to them is twenty years of ours. The summer for them is games and leisure, the winter is the country and a horse; time is slow and stretched over long hours. They write a page that should be immortal, but will not be; or they hammer out a lyric quite undistinguishable from its models, and yet to them a poignantly original thing.

Or am I all wrong? Is the world so rapidly changing that the Young also are caught with the obsession of change? Why, then, not even half the world is happy.

XVI

ETHANDUNE

In the parish of East Knoyle, in the county
of Wiltshire, and towards the western side of
that parish, there is an isolated knoll, gorse
covered, abrupt, and somewhat over 700 feet
above the sea in height. From the summit of it
a man can look westward, northward, and eastward over a great rising roll of countryside.

To the west, upon the sky-line of a level
range of hills, not high, runs that long wood
called Selwood and there makes an horizon. To
the north the cultivated uplands merge into
high open down: bare turf of the chalk, which
closes the view for miles against the sky, and is
the watershed between the Northern and the
Southern Avon. Eastward that chalk land falls
into the valley which holds Salisbury.

From this high knoll a man perceives the two
days' march which Alfred made with his levies

when he summoned the men of three Shires to fight with him against the Danes; he overthrew them at Ethandune.

The struggle of which these two days were the crisis was of more moment to the history of Britain and of Europe than any other which has imperilled the survival of either between the Roman time and our own.

That generation in which the stuff of society had worn most threadbare, and in which its continued life (individually the living memory of the Empire and informed by the Faith) was most in peril, was not the generation which saw the raids of the fifth century, nor even that which witnessed the breaking of the Mahommedan tide in the eighth, when the Christians carried it through near Poitiers, between the River Vienne and the Chain, the upland south of Chatellerault. The gravest moment of peril was for that generation whose grandfathers could remember the order of Charlemagne, and which fought its way desperately through the perils of the later ninth century.

ETHANDUNE

Then it was, during the great Scandinavian harry of the North and West, that Europe might have gone down. Its monastic establishment was shaken; its relics of central government were perishing of themselves; letters had sunk to nothing and building had already about it something nearly savage, when the swirl of the pirates came up all its rivers. And though legend had taken the place of true history, and though the memories of our race were confused almost to dreaming, we were conscious of our past and of our inheritance, and seemed to feel that now we had come to a narrow bridge which might or might not be crossed: a bridge already nearly ruined.

If that bridge were not crossed there would be no future for Christendom.

Southern Britain and Northern Gaul received the challenge, met it, were victorious, and so permitted the survival of all the things we know. At Ethandune and before Paris the double business was decided. Of these twin victories the first was accomplished in this island. Alfred is its hero, and its site is that chalk upland, above the Vale of Trowbridge, near which the second of the two white horses is carved: the hills above Eddington and Bratton upon the Westbury road.

The Easter of 878 had seen no King in England. Alfred was hiding with some small band in the marshes that lie south of Mendip against the Severn sea. It was one of those eclipses which time and again in the history of Christian warfare have just preceded the actions by which Christendom has re-arisen. In Whitsun week Alfred reappeared.

There is a place at the southern terminal of the great wood, Selwood, which bears a Celtic affix, and is called " Penselwood," " the head of the forest," and near it there stood (not to within living memory, but nearly so) a shirestone called Egbert's Stone; there Wiltshire, Somerset, and Dorset meet. It is just eastward of the gap by which men come by the south round Selwood into the open country, There the levies, that is the lords of Somerset

and of Wiltshire and their followers, come also
riding from Hampshire, met the King. But
many had fled over sea from fear of the Pagans.

" And seeing the King, as was meet, come to
life again as it were after such tribulations,
and receiving him, they were filled with an im-
mense joy, and there the camp was pitched."

Next day the host set out eastward to try its
last adventure with the barbarians who had
ruined half the West.

Day was just breaking when the levies set
forth and made for the uplands and for the
water partings. Not by mere and the marshes
of the valley, but by the great camp of White
Sheet and the higher land beyond it, the line
of marching and mounted men followed the
King across the open turf of the chalk to
where three Hundreds meet, and where the
gathering of the people for justice and the
courts of the Counts had been held before the
disasters of that time had broken up the land.

It was a spot bare of houses, but famous for
a tree which marked the junction of the Hun-

dreds. No more than three hundred years ago this tree still stood and bore the name of the Iley Oak. The place of that day's camp stands up above the water of Deveril, and is upon the continuation of that Roman road from Sarum to the Mendips and to the sea, which is lost so suddenly and unaccountably upon its issue from the great Ridge wood. The army had marched ten miles, and there the second camp was pitched.

With the next dawn the advance upon the Danes was made.

The whole of that way (which should be famous in every household in this country) is now deserted and unknown. The host passed over the high rolling land of the Downs from summit to summit until—from that central crest which stands above and to the east of Westbury—they saw before them, directly northward and a mile away, the ring of earthwork which is called to-day " Bratton Castle." Upon the slope between the great host of the pirates came out to battle. It was there from those naked heights that overlook the great plain of the Northern Avon, that the fate of England was decided.

The end of that day's march and action was the pressing of the Pagans back behind their earthworks, and the men who had saved our great society sat down before the ringed embankment watching all the gates of it, killing all the stragglers that had failed to reach that protection and rounding up the stray horses and the cattle of the Pagans.

That siege endured for fourteen days. At the end of it the Northmen treatied, conquered "by hunger, by cold, and by fear." Alfred took hostages "as many as he willed." Guthrum, their King, accepted our baptism, and Britain took that upward road which Gaul seven years later was to follow when the same anarchy was broken by Eudes under the walls of Paris.

All this great affair we have doubtfully followed to-day in no more than some three hundred words of Latin, come down doubtfully

over a thousand years. But the thing happened where and as I have said. It should be
as memorable as those great battles in which
the victories of the Republic established our
exalted but perilous modern day.

XVII

THE DEATH OF ROBERT THE STRONG

Up in the higher valley of the River Sarthe, which runs between low knolls through easy meadow-land, and is a place of cattle and of pasture, interspersed with woods of no great size, upon a summer morning a troop of some hundreds of men was coming down from the higher land to the crossings of the river. It was in the year 866. The older servants in the chief men's retinue could remember Charlemagne.

Two leaders rode before the troop. They were two great owners of land, and each possessed of commissions from the Imperial authority. The one had come up hastily northwards from Poitiers, the other had marched westward to join him, coming from the Beauce, with his command. Each was a *Comes*, a Lord

Administrator of a countryside and its capital, and had power to levy free men. Their retainers also were many. About them there rode a little group of aides, and behind them, before the footmen, were four squadrons of mounted followers.

The force had already marched far that morning. It was winding in line down a roughly beaten road between the growing crops of the hillside, and far off in the valley the leaders watched the distant villages, but they could see no sign of their quarry. They were hunting the pirates. The scent had been good from the very early hours when they had broken camp till lately, till mid-morning; but in the last miles of their marching it had failed them, and the accounts they received from the rare peasantry were confused.

They found a cottage of wood standing thatched near the track at the place where it left the hills for the water meadows, and here they recovered the trace of their prey. A wounded man, his right arm bound roughly with sacking, leaned against the door of the place, and with his whole left arm pointed at a group of houses more than a mile away beyond the stream, and at a light smoke which rose into the still summer air just beyond a screen of wood in its neighbourhood. He had seen the straggling line of the Northern men an hour before, hurrying over the Down and coming towards that farm.

Of the two leaders the shorter and more powerful one, who sat his horse the less easily, and whose handling of the rein was brutally strong, rode up and questioned and requestioned the peasant. Could he guess the numbers? It might be two hundred; it was not three. How long had they been in the countryside? Four days, at least. It was four days ago that they had tried to get into the monastery, near the new castle, and had been beaten off by the servants at the orchard wall. What damage had they done? He could not tell. The reports were few that he had heard. His cousin from up the valley complained that

three oxen had been driven from his fields by
night. They had stolen a chain of silver from
St. Giles without respect for the shrine. They
had done much more—how much he did not
know. Had they left any dead? Yes, three,
whom he had helped to bury. They had been
killed outside the monastery wall. One of his
fields was of the monastery benefice, and he had
been summoned to dig the graves.

The lord who thus questioned him fixed him
with straight soldierly eyes, and, learning no
more, rode on by the side of his equal from
Poitiers. That equal was armoured, but the
lord who had spoken to the peasant, full of
body and squat, square of shoulder, thick of
neck, tortured by the heat, had put off from
his chest and back his leather coat, strung with
rings of iron. His servant had unlaced it for
him some miles before, and it hung loose upon
the saddle hook. He had taken off, also, the
steel helm, and it hung by its strap to the same
point. He preferred to take the noon sun
upon his thick hair and to risk its action than

to be weighed upon longer by that iron. And this though at any moment the turn of a spinney might bring them upon some group of the barbarians.

Upon this short, resolute man, rather than upon his colleague, the expectation of the armed men was fixed. His repute had gone through all the North of Gaul with popular tales of his feats in lifting and in throwing. He was perhaps forty years of age. He boasted no lineage, but vague stories went about—that his father was from the Germanies; that his father was from the Paris land; that it was his mother who had brought him to court; that he was a noble with a mystery that forbade him to speak of his birth; that he was a slave whom the Emperor had enfranchised and to whom he had given favour; that he was a farmer's son; a yeoman.

On these things he had never spoken. No one had met men or women of his blood. But ever since his boyhood he had gone upwards in the rank of the empire, adding, also, one village to another in his possession, from the first which he had obtained no man knew how; purchasing land with the profits of office after office. He had been *Comes* of Tours, *Comes* of Auxerre, *Comes* of Nevers. He had the commission for all the military work between Loire and Seine. There were songs about him, and myths and tales of his great strength, for it was at this that the populace most wondered.

So this man rode by his colleague's side at the head of the little force, seeking for the pirates, when, unexpectedly, upon emerging from a fringe of trees that lined the flat meadows, his seat in the saddle stiffened and changed, and his eyes fired at what he saw. Two hundred yards before him was the stream, and over it the narrow stone bridge unbroken. Immediately beyond a group of huts and houses, wood and stone, and a heavy, low, round-arched bulk of a church marked the goal of the pirates—and there they were! They had seen the imperial levy the moment that it left the trees, and they were running—tall,

148

lanky men, unkempt, some burdened with sacks, most of them armed with battle-axe or short spear. They were making for cover in the houses of the village.

Immediately the two leaders called the marshallers of their levies, gave orders that the foot-men should follow, trotted in line over the bridge at the head of the squadron, and, once the water was passed, formed into two bodies of horse and galloped across the few fields into the streets of the place.

Just as they reached the market square and the front of the old church there, the last of the marauders (retarded under the weight of some burden he would save) was caught and pinned by a short spear thrown. He fell, crying and howling in a foreign tongue to gods of his own in the northland. But all his comrades were fast in the building, and there was a loud thrusting of stone statues and heavy furniture against the doors. Then, within a moment, an arrow flashed from a window slit, just missing one of the marshals. The Comes of Poitiers shouted for wood to burn the defence of the door, and villagers, misliking the task, were pressed. Faggots were dragged from sheds and piled against it. Even as this work was doing, man after man fell, as the defenders shot them at short range from within the church-tower.

The first of the foot-men had come up, and some half-dozen picked for marksmanship were attempting to thread with their whistling arrows the slits in the thick walls whence the bolts of the Vikings came. One such opening was caught by a lucky aim. For some moments its fire ceased, then came another arrow from it. It struck the Comes of Poitiers and he went down, and as he fell from his horse two servants caught him. Next, with a second shaft, the horse was struck, and it plunged and began a panic. No servant dared stab it, but a marshal did.

Robert, that second count, the leader, had dismounted. He was in a fury, mixed with the common men, and striking at the great church door blow upon blow, having in his hand a stone so huge that even at such a moment they marvelled at him.

Unarmoured, pouring with sweat, though at that western door a great buttress still shaded him from the noonday sun, Robert the Strong thundered enormously at the oak. A hinge broke, and he heard a salute of laughter from his men. He dropped his instrument, lifted, straining, a great beam which lay there, and trundled it like a battering-ram against the second hinge. But, just as the shock came, an arrow from the tower caught him also. It struck where the neck joins the shoulder, and he went down. Even as he fell, the great door gave, and the men of the imperial levy, fighting their way in, broke upon the massed pirates that still defended the entry with a whirl of axe and sword.

Four men tended the leader, one man holding his head upon his knee, the three others making shift to lift him, to take him where he might be tended. But his body was no longer convulsed; the motions of the arms had ceased;

and when the arrow was plucked at last from the wound, the thick blood hardly followed it. He was dead.

The name of this village and this church was Brissarthe; and the man who so fell, and from whose falling soldier songs and legends arose, was the first father of all the Capetians, the French kings.

From this man sprang Eudes, who defended Paris from the Sea-Rovers: Hugh Capet and Philip Augustus and Louis the Saint and Philip the Fair; and so through century after century to the kings that rode through Italy, to Henri IV, to Louis XIV in the splendour of his wars, and to that last unfortunate who lost the Tuileries on August 10th, 1793. His line survives to-day, for its eldest heir is the man whom the Basques would follow. His expectants call him Don Carlos, and he claims the crown of Spain.

XVIII

THE CROOKED STREETS

WHY do they pull down and do away with the Crooked Streets, I wonder, which are my delight, and hurt no man living?

Every day the wealthier nations are pulling down one or another in their capitals and their great towns: they do not know why they do it; neither do I.

It ought to be enough, surely, to drive the great broad ways which commerce needs and which are the life-channels of a modern city, without destroying all the history and all the humanity in between: the islands of the past. For, note you, the Crooked Streets are packed with human experience and reflect in a lively manner all the chances and misfortunes and expectations and domesticity and wonderment of men. One marks a boundary, another the kennel of an ancient stream, a third the track some animal took to cross a field hundreds upon hundreds of years ago; another is the line of an old defence, another shows where a rich man's garden stopped long before the first ancestor one's family can trace was born; a garden now all houses, and its owner who took delight in it turned to be a printed name.

Leave men alone in their cities, pester them not with the futilities of great governments, nor with the fads of too powerful men, and they will build you Crooked Streets of their very nature as moles throw up the little mounds or bees construct their combs. There is no ancient city but glories, or has gloried, in a whole foison and multitude of Crooked Streets. There is none, however wasted and swept by power which, if you leave it alone to natural things, will not breed Crooked Streets in less than a hundred years and keep them for a thousand more.

I know a dead city called Timgad, which the sand or the barbarians of the Atlas overwhelmed fourteen centuries ago. It lies between the desert and the Algerian fields, high up upon a mountain-side. Its columns stand. Even its fountains are apparent, though their waterways are choked. It has a great forum or market-place, all flagged and even, and the ruined walls of its houses mark its emplacement on every side. All its streets are straight, set out with a line, and by this you may judge how a Roman town lay when the last order of Rome sank into darkness.

Well, take any other town which has not thus been mummified and preserved but has lived through the intervening time, and you will find that man, active, curious, intense, in all the fruitful centuries of Christian time has endowed them with Crooked Streets, which kind of streets are the most native to Christian men. So it is with Arles, so it is with Nîmes, so it is with old Rome itself, and so it is with the City of London, on which by a special Providence the curse of the Straight Street has never fallen, so that it is to this day a labyrinth of little lanes. It was intended after the Great Fire to set it all out in order with " piazzas " and boulevards and the rest—but the English temper was too strong for any such nonsense, and the streets and the courts took to the natural lines which suit us best.

The Renaissance indeed everywhere began this plague of vistas and of avenues. It was determined three centuries ago to rebuild Paris as regular as a chessboard, and nothing but money saved the town—or rather the lack of money. You may to this day see in a square called the " Place des Vosges " what was intended. But when they had driven their Straight Street two hundred yards or so the exchequer ran dry, and thus was old Paris saved. But in the last seventy years they have hurt it badly again. I have no quarrel with what is regal and magnificent, with splendid ways of a hundred feet or more, with great avenues and lines of palaces; but why should they pull down my nest beyond the river— Straw Street and Rat Street and all those winding belts round the little Church of St.

THE CROOKED STREETS

Julien the Poor, where they say that Dante studied and where Danton in the madness of his grief dug up his dead love from the earth on his returning from the wars.

Crooked Streets will never tire a man, and each will have its character, and each will have a soul of its own. To proceed from one to another is like travelling in a multitude or mixing with a number of friends. In a town of Crooked Streets it is natural that one should be the Moneylenders' Street and another that of the Burglars, and a third that of the Politicians, and so forth through all the trades and professions.

Then also, how much better are not the beauties of a town seen from Crooked Streets! Consider those old Dutch towns where you suddenly come round a corner upon great stretches of salt water, or those towns of Central France which from one street and then another show you the Gothic in a hundred ways.

It is as it should be when you have the back of Chartres Cathedral towering up above you from between and above two houses gabled and almost meeting. It is what the builders meant when one comes out from such fissures into the great Place, the parvis of the cathedral, like a sailor from a river into the sea. Not that certain buildings were not made particularly for wide approaches and splendid roads, but that these, when they are the rule, sterilize and kill a town. Napoleon was wise enough when he designed that there should lead all up beyond the Tiber to St. Peter's a vast imperial way. But the modern nondescript horde, which has made Rome its prey, is very ill advised to drive those new Straight Streets foolishly, emptily, with mean facades of plaster and great gaps that will not fill.

You will have noted in your travels how the Crooked Streets gather names to themselves which are as individual as they, and which are bound up with them as our names are with all our own human reality and humour. Thus I bear in mind certain streets of the town where I served as a soldier. There was the Street of

the Three Little Heaps of Wheat, the Street of
the Trumpeting Moor, the Street of the False
Heart, and an exceedingly pleasant street called
"Who Grumbles at It?" and another short one
called "The Street of the Devil in His Haste,"
and many others.

From time to time those modern town coun-
cillors from whom Heaven has wisely withdrawn
all immoderate sums of money, and who therefore have not the power to take away my
Crooked Streets and put Straight ones in their
places, change old names to new ones. Every
such change indicates some snobbery of the
time: some little battle exaggerated to be a
great thing; some public fellow or other, in
Parliament or what not; some fad of the learned
or of the important in their day.

Once I remember seeing in an obscure corner
a twist of dear old houses built before George III
was king, and on the corner of this row
was painted "Kipling Street: late Nelson
Street."

Upon another occasion I went to a little

THE CROOKED STREETS

Norman market town up among the hills, where one of the smaller squares was called " The Place of the Three Mad Nuns," and when I got there after so many years and was beginning to renew my youth I was struck all of a heap to see a great enamelled blue and white affair upon the walls. They had renamed the triangle. They had called it " The Place Victor Hugo "!

However, all you who love Crooked Streets, I bid you lift up your hearts. There is no power on earth that can make man build Straight Streets for long. It is a bad thing, as a general rule, to prophesy good or to make men feel comfortable with the vision of a pleasant future; but in this case I am right enough. The Crooked Streets will certainly return.

Let me boldly borrow a quotation which I never saw until the other day, and that in another man's work, but which, having once seen it, I shall retain all the days of my life.

" Oh, passi graviora, dabit Deus his quoque

finem," or words to that effect. I can never be sure of a quotation, still less of scansion, and anyhow, as I am deliberately stealing it from another man, if I have changed it so much the better.

XIX

THE PLACE APART

LITTLE pen, be good and flow with ink (which you do not always do) so that I may tell you what came to me once in a high summer and the happiness I had of it.

.　　.　　.　　.　　.

One Summer morning as I was wandering from one house to another among the houses of men, I lifted up a bank from a river to a village and good houses, and there I was well entertained. I wish I could recite the names of those chance companions, but I cannot, for they did not tell me their names. June was just beginning in the middle lands where there are vines, but not many, and where the look of the stonework is still northern. The place was not very far from the Western Sea.

The bank on which the village stood above that river had behind it a solemn slope of woodland leading up gently to where, two miles or more away, yet not three hundred feet above me, the new green of the tree-tops made a line along the sky. Clouds of a little, happy, hurrying sort ran across the gentle blue of that heaven, and I thought, as I went onward into the forest upland, that I had come to very good things: but indeed I had come to things of a graver kind.

A path went on athwart the woods and upwards. This path was first regular, and then grew less and less marked, though it still preserved a clear-way through the undergrowth. The new leaves were opened all about me, and there was a little breeze: yet the birds piped singly and the height was lonely when I reached it, as though it were engaged in a sort of contemplation. At the summit was first one small clearing and then another, in which coarse grass grew high within the walls of trees; men had not often come that way, and those men only the few of the countryside.

Just where the slope began to go downwards

again upon the further side, these little clearings ceased and the woods closed in again. The path, or what was left of it, wholly failed, and I had now to push my way through many twigs and interlacing brambles, till in a little while that forest ceased abruptly upon the edge of a falling sward, and I saw before me the Valley.

Its floor must have lain higher than that river which I had crossed and left the same morning, for my ascent had been one of two miles or so, and my pushing downward on the further slope far less than one; moreover, that descent had been gentle.

The Valley opened to the right at my issue from the wood. To my left hand was a circle of the same trees as those through which I had passed, but to the right and so away northward, the pleasant empty dale.

Let me describe it.

Upon the further bank (for it was not steep enough to call a wall), the western bank which shut that valley in, grew a thick growth of low chestnuts with here and there a tall silver birch standing up among them. All this further slope was so held, and the chestnuts made a dark belt from which the tall graces of the birches lifted. The sunlight was behind that long afternoon of hills.

Opposite, the higher eastern slope stood full though gentle to the glorious light, and it was all a rise of pasture land. Its crest, which followed up and away northward for some miles, showed here and there a brown rock, aged and strong but low and half covered in the grass. These rocks were warm and mellow. The height of this eastern boundary was enough to protect the hollow below, but not so high as to carry any sense of savagery. It warned rather than forbade the approach of human kind. Between it and its opposing wooded fellow the narrowing floor of that Eden lay; winding, closing slowly, until it ended in a little cuplike pass, an easy saddle of grass where the two sides of the valley converged upon its northern conclusion. This pass was perhaps four miles away from me as I gazed, or perhaps a little less.

THE PLACE APART

The sun as I have said was shining upon all this: it made upon the little cuplike place a gentle shadow and a gentle light, both curved as the light might fall low and aslant upon a wooden bowl clothed in a soft green cloth. This was a lovely sight, and it invited me to go forward.

Therefore I went down the sward that fell from the abrupt edge of the wood, and set out to follow northward along the lower grasses of this single and most unexpected vale.

So strange was the place, even at this first sight, that I thought to myself: " I have happened upon one of those holidays God gives us." For we cannot give ourselves holidays: nor, if we are slaves, can our masters give us holidays, but God only: until at last we lay down the business and leave our work for good and all. And so much for holidays. Anyhow, the valley was a wonder to me there.

It was not as are common and earthly things. There was a peace about it which was not a mere repose, but rather something active which invited and intrigued. The meadows had a summons in them; and all was completely still. I heard no birds from the moment when I left the woodland, but a little brook, not shallow, ran past me for a companion as I went on. It made no murmur, but it slid full and at once mysterious and prosperous, brimming up to the rich field upon either side. I thought there must be chalk beneath it from its way of going. The pasture was not mown yet it was short, but if it had been fed there was no trace of herds anywhere; and indeed the grass was rather more in height than the grass of fed land, though it was not in flower. No wind moved it.

There were no divisions in this little kingdom; there were no walls or fences or hedges: it was all one field, with the woods upon the western slope to my left, and the tilted green of the eastern ridge to my right on which the sunlight softly and continually lay. Never have I found a place so much its own master and so contentedly alone.

THE PLACE APART

If any man owned that Valley, blessed be that man, but if no man owned it, and only God, then I could better understand the benediction which it imposed upon me, a chance wanderer, for something little less than an hour. Here was a place in which thought settled upon itself, and was not concerned with unanswerable things; and here was a place in which memory did not trouble one with the incompletion of recent trial, but rather stretched back to things so very old that all sense of evil had been well purged out of them. The ultimate age of the world which is also its youth, was here securely preserved. I was not so foolish as to attempt a prolongation of this blessedness: these things are not for possession: they are an earnest only of things which we may perhaps possess, but not while the business is on.

I went along at a good sober pace of travelling, taking care to hurt no blossom with my staff and to destroy no living thing, whether of leaves or of those that have movement.

So I went until I came to the low pass at

the head of the place, and when I had surmounted it I looked down a steep great fall into quite another land. I had come to a line where met two provinces, two different kinds of men, and this second valley was the end of one.

The moor (for so I would call it) upon the further side fell away and away distantly, till at its foot it struck a plain whereon I could see, further and further off to a very distant horizon, cities and fields and the anxious life of men.

169

XX

THE EBRO PLAIN

I WISH I could put before men who have not seen that sight, the abrupt shock which the Northern eye receives when it first looks from some rampart of the Pyrenees upon the new deserts of Spain.

" Deserts " is a term at once too violent and too simple. The effect of that amazement is by no means the effect which follows from a similar vision of the Sahara from the red-burnt and precipitous rocks of Atlas; nor is it the effect which those stretches of white blinding sand give forth when, looking southward toward Mexico and the sun, a man shades his eyes to catch a distant mark of human habitation along some rare river of Arizona from the cliff edge of a cut tableland.

Corn grows in that new Spain beneath one: many towns stand founded there; Christian

Churches are established; a human society stands firmly, though sparsely, set in that broad waste of land. But to the Northern eye first seeing it—nay, to a Northerner well acquainted with it, but returning to the renewal of so strange a vision—it is always a renewed perplexity how corn, how men, how worship, how society (as he has known them) can have found a place there; and that, although he knows that nowhere in Europe have the fundamental things of Europe been fought for harder and more steadfastly maintained than they have along this naked and burnt valley of the Ebro.

I will suppose the traveller to have made his way on foot from the boundaries of the Basque country, from the Peak of Anie, down through the high Pyrenean silences to those banks of Aragon where the river runs west between parallel ranges, each of which is a bastion of the main Pyrenean chain. I will suppose him to have crossed that roll of thick mud which the tumbling Aragon is in all these lower reaches, to have climbed the further range (which is called " The Mountains of Stone," or " The Mountains of the Rock "), and, coming upon its further southern slope, to see for the first time spread before him that vast extent of uniform dead-brown stretching through an air metallically clear to the tiny peaks far off on the horizon, which mark the springs of the Tagus. It is a characteristic of the stretched Spanish upland, from within sight of the Pyrenees to within sight of the Southern Sea, that it may thus be grasped in less than half a dozen views, wider than any views in Europe; and, partly from the height of that interior land, partly from the Iberian aridity of its earth, these views are as sharp in detail, as inhuman in their lack of distant veils and blues, as might be the landscapes of a dead world.

The traveller who should so have passed the high ridge and watershed of the Pyrenees, would have come down from the snows of the Anie through forests not indeed as plentiful as those of the French side, but still dignified by many

and noble trees, and alive with cascading water.
While he was yet crossing the awful barriers
(one standing out parallel before the next)
which guard the mountains on their Spainward
fall, he would continuously have perceived,
though set in dry, unhospitable soil, bushes and
clumps of trees; something at times resembling
his own Northern conception of pasture-land.
The herbage upon which he would pitch his
camp, the branches he would pick for firewood,
still, though sparse and Southern, would have
reminded him of home.

But when he has come over the furthest of
these parallel reaches, and sees at last the whole
sweep of the Ebro country spread out before
him, it is no longer so. His eye detects no
trees, save that belt of green which accompanies
the course of the river, no glint of water.
Though human habitation is present in that
landscape, it mixes, as it were, with the mud
and the dust of the earth from which it rose;
and, gazing at a distant clump in the plains
beneath him, far off, the traveller asks himself

doubtfully whether these hummocks are but small, abrupt, insignificant hills or a nest of the houses of men—things with histories.

For the rest all that immeasurable sweep of yellow-brown bare earth fills up whatever is not sky, and is contained or framed upon its final limit by mountains as severe as its own empty surface. Those far and dreadful hills are unrelieved by crag or wood or mist; they are a mere height, naked and unfruitful, running along wall-like and cutting off Aragon from the south and the old from the new Castile, save where the higher knot of the Moncayo stands tragic and enormous against the sky.

This experience of Spain, this first discovery of a thing so unexpected and so universally misstated by the pens of travellers and historians, is best seen in autumn sunsets, I think, when behind the mass of the distant mountains an angry sky lights up its unfruitful aspect of desolation, and, though lending it a colour it can never possess in commoner hours and seasons, in no way creates an illusion of fertility or of romance, of yield or of adventure, in that doomed silence.

The vision of which I speak does not, I know, convey this peculiar impression even to all of the few who may have seen it thus—and they are rare. They are rare because men do not now approach the old places of Europe in the old way. They come into a Spanish town of the north by those insufficient railways of our time. They return back home with no possession of great sights, no more memorable experience than of urban things done less natively, more awkwardly, more slowly than in England. Yet even those few, I say, who enter Spain from the north, as Spain should be entered— over the mountain roads—have not all of them received the impression of which I speak.

I have so received it, I know; I could wish that to the Northerner it were the impression most commonly conveyed: a marvel that men should live in such a place: a wonder when the ear catches the sound of a distant bell, that

ritual and a creed should have survived there—
so absolute is its message of desolation.

With a more familiar acquaintance this impression does not diminish, but increases.
Especially to one who shall make his way pain-
fully on foot for three long days from the
mountains to the mountains again, who shall toil
over the great bare plain, who shall cross by
some bridge over Ebro and look down, it may
be, at a trickle of water hardly moving in the
midst of a broad, stony bed, or it may be at a
turbid spate roaring a furlong broad after the
rains—in either case unusable and utterly un-
friendly to man; who shall hobble from little
village to little village, despairing at the silence
of men in that silent land and at their lack of
smiles and at the something fixed which watches
one from every wall; who shall push on over the
slight wheel-tracks which pass for roads—they
are not roads—across the infinite, unmarked,
undifferenced field; to one who has done all
these things, I say, getting the land into his
senses hourly, there comes an appreciation of

176

its wilful silence and of its unaccomplished soul. That knowledge fascinates, and bids him return. It is like watching with the sick who were thought dead, who are, in your night of watching, upon the turn of their evil. It is like those hours of the night in which the mind of some troubled sleeper wakened can find neither repose nor variety, but only a perpetual return upon itself—but waits for dawn. Behind all this lies, as behind a veil of dryness stretched from the hills to the hills, for those who will discover it, the intense, the rich, the unconquerable spirit of Spain.

XXI

THE LITTLE RIVER

MEN forget too easily how much the things they see around them in the landscapes of Britain are the work of men. Most of our trees were planted and carefully nurtured by man's hand. Our ploughs for countless centuries have made even the soil of the plains the lines of a great view; its groups of hedge and of building, of ridge and of road are very largely the creation of that curious and active breed which was set upon this dull round of the earth to enliven it—which, alone of creatures, speaks and has foreknowledge of death and wonders concerning its origin and its end. It is man that has transformed the surface and the outline of the old countries, and even the rivers carry his handiwork.

There is a little river on my land which very singularly shows the historical truth of what

THE LITTLE RIVER

I am here saying. As God made it, it was but a drain rambling through the marshy clay of tangled underwood, sluggishly feeling its way through the hollows in general weathers, scouring in a shapeless flood after the winter rains, dried up and stagnant in isolated pools in our hot summers. Then, no one will ever know how many centuries ago, man came, busy and curious, and doing with his hands. He took my little river; he began to use it, to make it, and to transform it, and to erect of it a human thing. He gave to it its ancient name, which is the ancient name for water, and which you will find scattered upon streams large and small from the Pyrenees up to the Northern Sea and from the West of Germany to the Atlantic. He called it the Adur; therefore pedants pretend that the name is new and not old, for pedants hate the fruitful humour of antiquity.

Well, not only did man give my little river (an inconceivable number of generations ago) the name which it still bears, but he bridged it and he banked it, he scoured it and he dammed it, until he made of it a thing to his own purpose and a companion of the country-side.

With the fortunes of man in our Western and Northern land the fortunes of my little river rose and fell. What the Romans may have done with it we do not know, for a clay soil preserves but little—coins sink in it and the foundations of buildings are lost.

In the breakdown which we call the Dark Ages, and especially perhaps after the worst business of the Danish Invasion, it must have broken back very nearly to the useless and un-profitable thing it had been before man came. The undergrowth, the little oaks and the maples, the coarse grass, the thistle patches, and the briars encroached upon tilled land; the banks washed down, floods carried away the rotting dams, the waterwheels were forgotten and perished. There seem to have been no mills. There is no good drinking water in that land, save here and there at a rare spring, unless you dig a well, and the people of the Dark Ages in

Britain, broken by the invasion, dug no wells in the desolation of my valley.

Then came the Norman: the short man with the broad shoulders and the driving energy, and that regal sense of order which left its stamp wherever he marched, from the Grampians to the Euphrates. He tamed that land again, he ploughed the clay, he cut the undergrowth, and he built a great house of monks and a fine church of stone where for so long there had been nothing but flying robbers, outlaws, and the wolves of the weald.

To my little river the Norman was particularly kind. He dug it out and deepened it, he bridged it again and he sluiced it; it brimmed to its banks, it was once more the companion of men, and, what is more, he dug it out so thoroughly all the twenty miles to the sea that he could even use it for barges and for light boats, so that this head of the stream came to be called Shipley, for goods of ships could be floated, when all this was done, right up to the wharf which the Knight Templars had built above the church to meet the waters of the stream.

All the Middle Ages that fruitfulness and that use continued. But with the troubles in which the Middle Ages closed and in which so much of our civilisation was lost, the little river was once more half abandoned. The church still stood, but stone by stone the great building of the Templars disappeared. The river was no longer scoured; its course was checked by dense bush and reed, the wild beasts came back, the lands of the King were lost. One use remained to the water—the Norman's old canalisation was forgotten and the wharf had slipped into a bank of clay, and was now no more than a tumbled field with no deep water standing by. This use was the use of the Hammer Ponds. Here and there the stream was banked up, and the little fall thus afforded was used to work the heavy hammers of the smithies in which the iron of the countryside was worked. For in this clay of ours there was ironstone everywhere, and the many oaks of the weald furnished the charcoal for its smelting. The metal work of the great ships that fought the French, many of their guns also, and bells and railings for London, were smithied or cast at the issue of these Hammer Ponds. But coal came and the new smelting; our iron was no longer worked, and the last usefulness of the little river seemed lost.

Then for two generations all that land lay apart, the stream quite choked or furiously flooding, the paths unworkable in winter: no roads, but only green lanes, and London, forty miles away, unknown.

The last resurrection of the little river has begun to-day. The railway was the first bringer of good news (if you will allow me to be such an apologist for civilisation); then came good hard roads in numbers, and quite lately the bicycle, and, last of all, the car. The energy of men reached Adur once again, and once again began the scouring and making of the banks and the harnessing of the water for man; so that, though we have not tackled the canal as we should (that will come), yet with every year the Adur grows more and more of a companion again. It has furnished two fine great lakes for two of my neighbours, and in one place after another they have bridged it as they should, and though clay is a doubtful thing to deal with they have banked it as well.

The other day as I began a new and great and good dam with sluices and with puddled clay behind oak boards and with huge oak uprights and oaken spurs to stand the rush of the winter floods, I thought to myself, working in that shimmering and heated air, how what I was doing was one more of the innumerable things that men had done through time incalculable to make the river their own, and the thought gave me great pleasure, for one becomes larger by mixing with any company of men, whether of our brothers now living or of our fathers who are dead.

This little river—the river Adur before I have done with it—will be as charming and well-bred a thing as the Norman or the Roman knew. It shall bring up properly to well-cut banks. These shall be boarded. It shall have clear depths of water in spite of the clay, and reeds and water lilies shall grow only where I choose. In every way it shall be what the things of this world were made to be—the servant and the instrument of Man.

XXII

SOME LETTERS OF SHAKE-SPEARE'S TIME

From Lord Mulberry to his sister, Mrs. Blake

MY DEAR VICTORIA,—Yes, by all means tell your young friend Mr. Shakespeare that he can come to Paxton on Saturday. As you say that he can't get away until the later train I will have Perkins meet him from the village. I don't suppose he rides, but I can't mount him anyhow. I hope there is no trouble about Church on Sunday.

From Mrs. Myers to Lady Clogg

One thing I *am* looking forward to, dear, is this little coon Shakespeare. Victoria told me about him. She says sometimes he will play and sometimes he won't play. But *she* says he's quiet in harness just now. It seems that sometimes he talks all of a sudden. And one

186

can get him to *sing!* Anyhow I *do* want to see what he's like.

(*The rest of this letter is about other matters.*)

From Messrs. Hornbull and Sons to William Shakespeare Esq.

SIR,—We have now sent in our account three times, and the last time with a pressing recommendation that you should settle it, but you have not honoured us by any reply. We regret to inform you that if we do not receive a cheque by Wednesday the 22nd inst. we shall be compelled to put the matter into other hands.

From John Shakespeare to his mother, Mrs. Shakespeare

DEAREST MAMMA,—I am afraid Billie really can't pay that money this week. He was awfully apologetic about it and I gave him a good talking to, but if he hasn't got it he hasn't. After all it isn't absolutely necessary until the 30th.

IN SHAKESPEARE'S TIME

*From Jonathan Truelove Esq. to William
Shakespeare Esq,*

DEAR OLD CHAP,—I am going to do something very unconventional, but we know each
other well enough I think. Can you let me have
the £5 I lent you two years ago? I have to get
in every penny I can this week, suddenly. If
you can't don't bother to answer, I am not
going to press you.

*From Sir Henry Portman, Attorney General,
to the Secretary of the Crown Prosecutor*

DEAR JIM,—No, I can't manage to get round
to the Ritz this evening. Mary says that she
wants Johnnie to leave Dresden. What inconceivable rubbish! Why can't she let him stay
where he is? You might as well drown yourself as leave Dresden. What on earth could it
lead to?

By the way, do choke off that silly ass Bates,
if he is still worrying about Shakespeare. No
one wants anything done, and No. 1 would be
awfully angry if there was a prosecution.

Rather than allow it I would find the money myself.

Yours,   H. P.

From James Jevons and Co. Publishers, to William Shakespeare Esq.

DEAR SIR,—Our attention has been called to your work by our correspondent in Edinburgh, and he asks us whether we think you could see your way to something dealing with Scottish history. He does not want it cast in the form of a play, for which he says there will be no sale with the Scottish public, seeing the exceedingly English cast of your work, but if you could throw it into Ballad form he thinks something could be done with it.

Of course such things can never be remunerative at *first*. The Edinburgh firm for whom he writes propose to buy sheets at 4½d. or 5d. and to give a royalty of 10 per cent. to be equally divided between our firm and yourself. They could not go beyond 500 copies for the first edition. It may be worth your while, in spite

189

of the trifling remuneration, to consider this offer in order to secure copyright and to prevent any pirating of future editions in Scotland. Pray advise.

>We are,

>>Your obedient servants,

>>>JAMES JEVONS AND Co.

From Messrs. Firelight, Agents, to William Shakespeare Esq.

DEAR MR. SHAKESPEARE,—We have had a proposal from Messrs. Capon in the matter of your collected Poems. As you know, verse is not just now much in demand with the public, and they could not manage an advance on royalties. They propose 10 per cent. on a 5s. book after the first 250 copies sold. The honorarium is, of course, purely nominal, but it might lead to more business later on. Could you let us know your views upon the matter?

>Very faithfully yours,

>>*pro* FIRELIGHT AND Co.

>>>C. G.

IN SHAKESPEARE'S TIME

From Clarence de Vere Chalmondeley to William Shakespeare Esq.

DEAR SIR,—Having certain sums free for investment, I am prepared to lend, not as a money-lender but as a private banker, sums from £10 to £50,000, on note of hand alone, without security. No business done with minors.

Very faithfully yours,

CLARENCE DE VERE CHALMONDELEY.

From William Shakespeare to Sir John Fowless (scribbled hastily in pencil)

I will try and come if I can, but it's something awful. I only got my proofs read by 2 o'clock in the night; I had to do my article for *The Owl* before 10 this morning, then I have got to go and meet the Church Defence League people on my way to the station, and catch a train to a place where Mrs. Blake wants me to go somewhere in the Midlands, about 5. I think I can look in on my way to the station.

191

IN SHAKESPEARE'S TIME

That man you asked me to see about the brandy is a fraud. Would you, like a good fellow, tell Charlie *not to forget to mention in his article that " Hamlet " will only be played on Tuesdays and Fridays in the afternoon, matinées.* Don't forget this because people want to know when it is going to be. There was a very good notice in *The Jumper.* I do feel so ill.

W. S.

From S. Jennings, Secretary, to
George Mountebank Esq.

Dear Sir,—Mr. Shakespeare is at present away from home and will return upon Thursday, when I will immediately lay your MSS. before him.

I am,

Very faithfully yours,

S. Jennings, Secretary.

IN SHAKESPEARE'S TIME

From Mr. Mustwrite of Warwick to
William Shakespeare Esq.

DEAR MR. SHAKESPEARE,—I have never met
you, and perhaps you will think it a great im-
pertinence on my part to be writing as I do.
But I must write to tell you the deep and sincere
pleasure I have received from your little
brochure " Venus and Adonis," which the Rev.
William Clarke, our Clergyman, lent me only
yesterday. I read it through at a sitting and I
could not rest until I had written to tell you
the profound spiritual consolation I derived
from its perusal.

I am, dear Mr. Shakespeare,

Very much your admirer,

GEORGE MUSTWRITE.

To William Shakespeare Esq. (unsigned, and
written in capital letters rather irregularly)

No doubt you think yourself a fine fellow and
the friend of the working man—I don't think!
Some of us know more about you than you think

we do. I erd you at the Queen's Hall and you made me sick. You aren't fit to black the boots of the man you talked against.

To William Shakespeare Esq., O.H.M.S.
(printed)

Sir,—In pursuance with the provisions of Her Majesty's Benevolent Act, you are hereby required to prepare a true and correct statement of your emoluments from all forms of (in writing) literary income, duly signed by you within 21 days from this date. If, however, you elect to be assessed by the District Commissioners under a number or a letter, &c. &c. &c.

From the Earl of Essex to W. Shakespeare Esq.
(lithographed)

Dear Sir,—I have undertaken to act as Chairman this year of the Annual Dinner of the League for the Support of Insufficiently Talented Dramatic Authors. You are doubtless acquainted with the admirable objects of

194

IN SHAKESPEARE'S TIME

&c. &c. I hope I may see your name among the stewards whose position is purely honorary, and is granted upon payment of five guineas, &c. &c. This laudable &c. &c.

Very faithfully yours,

Essex.

From Mrs. Parxinson to William Shakespeare Esq.

DEAR MR. SHAKESPEARE,—Can you come and talk for our Destitute Pick Pockets Association on Thursday the 18th? I know you are a very busy man, but I always find it is the most busy men, who somehow manage to find time for charitable objects. If you can manage to do so I would send my motor round for you to Pilbury Row, and it would take you out to Rickmansworth where the meeting is to be. I am afraid it cannot take you back, but there is a convenient train at 20 minutes to 8, which gets you into London a little after 9 for dinner, or, if that is too late you might catch the 6.30, which gets you in at 8.15, only that will be rather a rush. My daughter tells me how much she admired your play, *Macduff*, and very much wants to see you.

From the Duchess of Dump to William Shakespeare Esq.

DEAR MR. SHAKESPEARE,—I want to ask you a really *great* favour. Could you come to my Animals Ball on the 4th of June dressed up as a gorilla? I *do* hope you can. We have to tell people what costumes they are to wear for fear that they should duplicate. Now *don't* say no. It's years since we met. Last February wasn't it?

Yours ever,

CAROLINE DUMP.

Printed on Blue Paper with the Royal Arms

In the name of the Queen's grace, OYEZ!

WHEREAS there has appeared before Us Henry Holt a Commissioner of the Queen's, &c. &c.

AND WHEREAS the said Henry Holt maketh

deposition that he has against you (*in writing*) *William Shakespeare*, a claim for the sum of (*in writing*) *£27 2s. 1d.*, now we hereby notify you that you are summoned to appear before us, &c. &c., upon (*in writing*) *Wednesday the 25th of May* in the Year of Our Lord (*in writing*) *1601*, given under the Common Seal this (*in writing*) *second day of May 1601*.

HENRY HOLT, a Commissioner of the Queen's &c. &c.

XXIII

ON ACQUAINTANCE WITH THE GREAT

IT is generally recognised in this country that an acquaintance more or less familiar with the Great, that is, with the very wealthy, and preferably with those who have been wealthy for at least one generation, is the proper entry into any form of public service.

I am in a position to advance for the benefit of younger men of my own social rank, certain views which I think will not be unprofitable to them in this matter.

I will suppose my reader to be still upon the right side of thirty; to be the son of some professional man; to have been kept, at the expense of some anxiety to his parents, for five years or so at a public school, and to have proceeded to the University upon a loan.

With such a start he cannot fail, if he is in

any way lively or amiable, to have made the acquaintance by the age of twenty-two of a whole group of men whose fathers may properly be called " The Great," and who themselves will inherit a similar distinction, unless they die prematurely of hard living or hereditary disease.

After such a beginning, common to many of my readers, the friendship and patronage of these people would seem to be secure; and yet we know from only too many fatal instances that it is nothing of the kind, and that of twenty young men who have scraped up acquaintance with their betters at Winchester or Magdalen (to take two names at random) not two are to be found at the age of forty still familiarly entering those London houses, which are rated at over £1000 a year.

The root cause of such failures is obvious enough.

The advantage of acquaintance with wealthy or important people would, so far as general opportunities go, be lost if one did not advertise it; and here comes in a difficulty which has wrecked innumerable lives. For by a pretty paradox with which we are all of us only too well acquainted, the wealthy and important are particularly averse to the recitation of acquaintance with themselves.

Formerly—about seventy years ago—your man who would succeed recited upon the slightest grounds, in public and with emphasis, his friendship with the Great. It was one of Disraeli's methods of advancement. The Great discovered the crude method, denounced it, vilified it, and towards the year 1860 it had already become impossible. William tells me he remembers his dear father warning me of this.

Those who would advance in the next generation were compelled to abandon methods so simple and to take refuge in allusion. Thus a young fellow in the late sixties, the seventies, and the very early eighties was helped in his career by professing a profound dislike for such and such a notability and swearing that he would not meet him. For to profess dislike was to profess familiarity with the world in which that notability moved.

Or, again, to analyse rather curiously, and, on the whole, unfavourably, the character of some exceedingly wealthy man, was a method that succeeded well enough in hands of average ability. While a third way was to use Christian names, and yet to use them with a tone of indifference, as though they belonged to acquaintances rather than friends.

But the Great are ever on the alert, and this habit of allusion was in its turn tracked down by their unfailing noses; so that in our own time it has been necessary to invent another. I do not promise it any long survival, I write only for the moment, and for the fashions of my time, but I think a young man is well advised in this second decade of the twentieth century to assume towards the Great an attitude of silent and sometimes weary familiarity, and very often to pretend to know them less well than he does.

Thus three men will be in a smoking room together. The one, let us say, will be the Master of the King's Billiard Room, an aged Jew who has lent money to some Cabinet Minister; the second a local squire, well-to-do and about fifty years of age; the third is my young reader, whose father, let us say, was a successful dentist. The Master of the King's Billiard Room will say that he likes " Puffy." The squire will say he doesn't like him much because of such and such a thing; he will ask the young man for his opinion. Now, in my opinion, the young man will do well at this juncture to affect ignorance. Let him deliberately ask to have it explained to him who Puffy is (although the nickname may be familiar to every reader of a newspaper), and on hearing that it is a certain Lord Patterson he should put on an expression of no interest, and say that he has never met Lord Patterson.

Something of the same effect is produced when a man remains silent during a long conversation about a celebrity, and then towards the end of it says some really true and intimate thing about him, such as, that he rides in long stirrups, or that one cannot bear his double eyelids or that his gout is very amusing.

Another very good trick, which still possesses great force, is to repudiate any personal acquaintance with the celebrity in question, and treat him merely as some one whom one has read of in the newspapers; but next, as though following a train of thought, to begin talking of some much less distinguished relative of his with the grossest possible familiarity.

A common and not ineffective way (which I mention to conclude the list) is to pretend that you have only met the Great Man in the way of business, at large meetings or in public places, where he could not possibly remember you, and to pretend this upon all occasions and very often. But this method is only to be used when, as a matter of fact, you have not met the celebrity at all.

As for letting yourself be caught unawares and showing a real and naïf ignorance of the

Great, that is not only a fault against which I will not warn you, for I believe you to be incapable of it, but it is also one against which it is of no good to warn any one, for whoever commits it has no chance whatsoever of that advancement which it is the object of these notes to promote.

When you are found walking with the Great in the street (a thing which, as a rule, they feel a certain shyness in doing, at least in company with people of your position), it is as well, if your companion meets another of his own Order, to stand a little to one side, to profess interest in the objects of a neighbouring shop window, or the pattern of the railings. Such at least is the general rule to be laid down for those who have not the quickness or ability to seize at once the better method, which is as follows:

Catch if you can the distant approach of the Other Great before your Great has spotted him, then, upon some pretext, preferably accompanied by the pulling out of your watch, depart:

for there is nothing that so annoys the Great during the conference of any two of them, as the presence of a third party of your station.

Since my remarks must be put into a brief compass (though I have much more to say upon this all-important subject) I will conclude with what is perhaps the soundest piece of advice of all.

Never under any occasion or temptation, bestow a gift even of the smallest value, upon the Great. Never let yourself be betrayed into a generous action, nor, if you can possibly prevent it, so much as a generous thought in their regard. They are not grateful. They think it impertinent. And it looks odd. There is a note of equality about such things (and this particularly applies to unbosoming yourself in correspondence) which is very odious and offensive. Moreover, as has been proved in the case of countless unhappy lives, when once a man of the middle class falls into the habit of asking the Great to meals, of giving them books or pictures or betraying towards them in any fashion a spirit of true companionship, he bursts; and that, as a rule, after a delay quite incredibly short. Some men of fair substance have to my knowledge been wholly ruined in this manner within the space of one parliamentary session, a hunting season, or even a single week at Cowes, in the Isle of Wight; from which spot I send these presents, and where, by the way, at the time of writing, the stock of forage in the forecastle is extremely low, with no supplies forthcoming from the mainland.

God bless you!

XXIV

ON LYING

He that will set out to lie without having cast up his action and judged it this way and that, will fail, not in his lie, indeed, but in the object of it; which is, *imprimis*, to deceive, but *in ultimis* or fundamentally, to obtain profit by his deceit, as Aristotle and another clearly show. For they that lie, lie not vainly and wantonly as for sport (saving a very few that are habitual), but rather for some good to be got or evil to be evaded: as when men lie of their prowess with the fist, though they have fought none—no, not even little children—or in the field, though they have done no more than shoot a naked blackamoor at a furlong. These lie for honour. Not so our stockers and jobbers, who lie for money direct, or our parliament men, who lie bestraught lest worse befall them.

207

ON LYING

Lies are distinguished by the wise into the Pleasant and the Useful, and again into the Beautiful and the Necessary. Thus a lie giving comfort to him that utters it is of the Lie Pleasant, a grateful thing, a cozening. This kind of lies is very much used among women. This sort will also make out good to the teller, evil to the told, for the pleasure the cheat gives; as, when one says to another that his worst actions are now known and are to be seen printed privately in a Midland sheet, and bids him fly.

The lie useful has been set out *ut supra,* which consult; and may be best judged by one needing money. Let him ask for the same and see how he shall be met; all answers to him shall be of this form of lie. It is also of this kind when a man having no purse or no desire to pay puts sickness on in a carriage, whether by rail or in the street, crying out: " Help! help! " and wagging his head and sinking his chin upon his breast, while his feet patter and his lips dribble. Also let him roll his eyes. Then some will say: "It is the heat! The poor fellow is overcome!" Others, "Make way! make way!" Others, men of means, will ask for the police, whereat the poorer men present will make off. But chiefly they that should have taken the fare will feel kindly and will lift the liar up gently and convey him and put him to good comfort in some waiting place or other till he be himself—and all the while clean forget his passage. For such is the nature of their rules. Lord Hincksey, now dead, was very much given to this kind of lie, and thought it profitable.

You shall lie at large and not be discovered; or a little, and for once, and yet come to public shame, as it was with Ananias and his good wife Sapphira in Holy Scripture, who lied but once and that was too often. While many have lied all their lives long and come to no harm, like John Ade, of North-Chapel, for many years a witness in the Courts that lied professionally, then a money-lender, and lastly a parliament-man for the county: yet he had no hurt of all this that any man could see, but died easily in another man's bed, being eighty-three years of age or thereabouts, and was very honourably buried in Petworth at a great charge. But some say he is now in Hell, which God grant!

There is no lie like the winsome, pretty, flattering, dilating eyelid-and-lip-and-brow-lifting lie such as is used by beauty impoverished, when land is at stake. By this sort of lie many men's estates have been saved, none lost, and good done at no expense save to holiness. Of the same suit also is the lie that keeps a parasite in a rich man's house, or a mixer attendant upon a painter, a model upon a sculptor, and beggars upon all men.

Fools will believe their lies, but wise men also will take delight in them, as did the Honourable Mr. Gherkin, for some time His Majesty's Minister of State for the Lord Knows What, who, when policemen would beslaver him, and put their hands to their heads and pay court in a low way, told all that saw it what mummery it was; yet inwardly was pleased. The more at a loss was he when, being by an accident in the Minories too late and his hat lost, his coat torn and muddy, he made to accost an officer, and civilly saying, " Hi——" had got no further but he took such a crack on the crown with a truncheon as laid him out for dead, and he is not now the same as he was, nor ever will be.

Ministers of religion will both show forth to the people the evil of lying and will also lie themselves in a particular manner, very distinct and formidable: as was clear when one denounced from the pulpit the dreadful vice of hypocrisy and false seeming, whereat a drunkard not yet sober, hearing him say, " Show me the hypocrite! " rose where he was, full in church, and pointed to the pulpit, so that he was thrust out for truth-telling by gesture in that sacred place; as was that other who, when the preacher came to " Show me the drunkard," jerked his thumb over his shoulder at the parson's wife: a very mutinous act. But to Lying.

He that takes lying easily will take life hardly; as the saw has it, " Easy lying makes hard hearing," but your constructed and considered, your well-drafted lie—that is the lie for men grown, men discreet and fortunate. To which effect also the poet Shakespeare says in his *Sonnets*—but no matter! The passage is not for our ears or time, dealing with a dark woman that would have her Will: as women also must if the world is to wag, which leads me to that sort of lie common to all the sex of which we men say that it is the marvellous, the potent, the dextrous, the thorough, or better still, the mysterious, the uncircumvented and not explainable, the stopping-short and confounding-against-right-reason lie, the triumphant lie of Eve our mother: Iseult our sister: Judith, an aunt of ours, who saved a city, and Jael, of holy memory.

But if any man think to explain that sort of lie, he is an ass for his pains; and if any man seek to copy it he is an ass sublimate or compound, for he attempts the mastery of women.

Which no man yet has had of God, or will.

Amen.

XXV

THE DUPE

THE Dupe is an honest creature, and such honesty is the noblest work of God. The Dupe is not the servant of the Knave, but his ally. The Dupe does not, as too simple a political philosophy would have it, serve only for a material on which the Knave shall work; he is also the moral support of the Knave, strengthening and comforting the Knave's most inward soul and lending lubrication to the friction of public falsehood. For the Knave is of many sorts, and the Dupe helps them all.

The plumb Knave, or Knave Absolute, finds in the Dupe such an honest creature as does not revile him, and it is good to know that one is loved by some few honest souls. Thus the Knave Absolute is foolish indeed when he lets the Dupe see by gesture or tone that he thinks him a fool, for the Dupe is very sensitive and touchy in all weathers.

The Knave Qualified (in his many incarnations) must have the Dupe about him or perish. Thus the Knave who would save his soul by self-deception feeds, cannibal-like, upon the straightforwardness of the Dupe, and says to himself: "How can I be such a Knave after all, since these good Dupes here heartily agree with me?"

The Knave Cowardly props himself upon that that sort of courage in the Dupe which always accompanies virtue. "I run a risk," says he, "in proposing the State purchase of this or that at such and such a price. My friend the Old Knave went under thus in 1895; but the Good Dupe is a buckler in the fight; he will dare all because his heart is pure."

The Knave Slovenly looks to the Dupe to see to details and to meet men in ante-chambers, and to have kind, honest eyes in bargaining. This sort of Knave will have two or even three Dupes for private secretaries, and often one for a brother-in-law.

THE DUPE

The Dupe is in God's providence very numerous, for his normal rate of breeding is high in the extreme, his normal death-rate low. On this account those curious in this part of natural history may watch the Dupes going about in great herds, conducted and instructed by the Knave; nor is the one to be distinguished from the other by the coat, but rather by the snout and visage, the eyes and, if one be old enough to open the mouth, by the teeth. The Dupe, upon the other hand, will not be of great service in any physical struggle and must not be depended upon for this. It is his delight to browse and when disturbed he scatters rather than flies. Here and there a Rogue Dupe will turn upon his pursuers, in which case he is invariably devoured.

The Dupe has his habitat, but that not easily defined, as in the suburbs of great cities, and in those towns called residential, where the leisured and the inane make their lives seem so much longer than those of others. But there are exceptions also to this, and the Dupe will some-

215

times migrate in vast numbers from one spot to another in such few years as wholly to discomfit the calculations of the Knaves. Some of these have been found to stand up in public halls before numbers whom they had thought to be Dupes (seeing that the locality was Little Partington) but only to discover a great boiling of Anti-Dupes, men working with their hands or what-not, quite undeceivable, as often as not Atheist, and ready to storm the platform and tear the Knave alive.

The Dupe loves courtesy and, as has been said above, will tolerate no hint of impatience. On the other hand, he needs no breaking in and will carry upon the back from his earliest years. It is incredible to travellers when they first come across the Dupe what burdens he will bear in this fashion, so that sometimes the whole Plain appears to be a moving mass of gold bags, public salaries, contracts, large houses, yachts, motor-cars, opera houses, howdahs sheltering masters and mistresses, cases of wine, rich foods, and charitable institutions, all as it were endowed with a motion of their own until you stoop down and perceive that the whole of this vast weight sways securely upon the backs of an enormous migratory body of Dupes upon the trek for a Better Land.

The Dupe also differs from other creatures in that he will sleep comfortably with such things upon his back, nor ever roll over upon them, and that he will bear them to a great old age and even to death itself without dispute. Indeed the Dupe unburdened has about him a forlorn and naked feeling to which it were a pity to condemn him. His food must be ample, but there is no need to prepare it carefully, and he will eat almost anything that is given him, except a leek, which he will not touch unless he be told that it is an onion. Of wheat he takes very little, but he insists that a great portion be put before him, that he may munch and trample upon it. Why he manifests this appetite is not known, but upon any attempt to lessen the ration he will kick, buck, and rear, and behave in a manner altogether out of his nature.

The Dupe must be given drink at irregular intervals, but he loves to treat it shyly, and to flirt with it as it were. There is no prettier sight than to see a number of Dupes met together arching and curvetting, side-glancing and denying, before they plunge their heads and manes into the life-giving liquid.

It is the reward of the Dupe that he is all his life very consistently happy, and on this account many not born Dupes, imitate the Dupes and would be of them, in which they fail, for the Dupe is God's creature and not man's, and proceeds by moral generation as has already been affirmed.

XXVI

THE LOVE OF ENGLAND

Love of country is general to mankind, yet is not the love of country a general thing to be described by a general title. Love changes with the object of love. The country loved determines the nature of its services.

The love of England has in it the love of landscape, as has the love of no other country: it has in it as has the love of no other country, the love of friends. Less than the love of other countries has it in it the love of what may be fixed in a phrase or well set down in words. It lacks, alas, the love of some interminable past nor does it draw its liveliness from any great succession of centuries. Say that ten centuries made a soil, and that in that soil four centuries more produced a tree, and that that tree was England, then you will know to what the love of England is in most men directed. For most

men who love England know so little of her first
thousand years that when they hear the echoes
of them or see visions of them, they think they
are dealing with a foreign thing. All Englishmen are clean cut off from their long past which
ended when the last Mass was sung at Westminster.

The love of England has in it no true plains
but fens, low hills, and distant mountains. No
very ancient towns, but comfortable, small and
ordered ones, which love to dress themselves with
age. The love of England concerns itself with
trees. Accident has given to the lovers of
England no long pageantry of battle. Nature
has given Englishmen an appetite for battle,
and between the two men who love England
make a legend for themselves of wars unfought,
and of arms permanently successful; though
arms were they thus always successful would not
be arms at all.

The greatness of the English soul is best
discovered in that strong rebuke of excesses,
principally of excess in ignorance, which a

minority of Englishmen perpetually express, but which has not sufficed as yet to save the future of England. In no other land will you so readily discover critics of that land ready to bear all for their right to doubt the common policy; but though you will nowhere discover such men so readily, nowhere will you discover them so impotent or so few.

The love of England breeds in those who cherish it an attachment to institutions which is half reverential, but also half despairing. In its reverence this appetite produces one hundred living streams of action and of vesture and of custom. In its despair, in its refusal to consider upon what theory the institution lies, it permits the institution to sterilise with age and to grow fantastic.

The love of England has never destroyed, but at times, and again at closer and at closer times (while we have lived) it has failed to save. Yet it will save England in the end. Men are more bound together by this music in their souls than by any other, wherever England is or is spoken of by Englishmen. Here you may discover what religion has been to many, and also you may discover here how legend and how epics arise. In men cut off from England, the love of England grows into a set repetitive thing, a thing of peculiar strength yet almost barren. Nourished and exampled by England, flourishing upon the field of England, the love of England is a love of the very earth: of the smell of growing things and of certain skies, and of tides in river-mouths, and of belts of sea.

If a man would understand this great thing England which is now in peril and which has so worked throughout the world, he must not consider the accident of England's success and failure, nor certain empty lands filled without battle, nor others ruined by folly, nor certain arts singularly discovered and perfected by England, nor other arts as singularly neglected and decayed. Nor must he contrast the passionate love of England with some high religion of which it takes the place, nor with some active work in contrast with which it seems so empty and unproducing a thing. He must not set it against a creed (it is not so high as that), nor against a conquest or a true empire such as Spain and Rome possessed.

If a man would understand the love of England he must do what hardly any one would dare to do: that is, he must clearly envisage England defeated in a final war and ask himself, " What should I do then? "

XXVII

THE STORM

THERE is a contemptible habit of mind (contemptible in intellect, not in morals) which would withdraw from the mass of life the fecundity of perception.

The things that we see are, according to the interpretation of the mystics, every one of them symbols and masks of things unseen.   The mystics have never proved their theory true.   But it is undoubtedly true that the perception of things when it is sane is manifold; it is true that as we grow older the perception of things is increasingly manifold, and that one perception breeds one hundred others, so that we advance through life as through a pageant enjoying in greater and greater degree day by day (if we open ourselves to them) the glorious works of God.

There is a detestable habit of mind, which

either does not understand, or sneers at, or despises, or even wholly misses—when it is persisted in—this faculty for enjoyment, which even our gross senses endow us with. This evil habit of the mind will have us neglect first colour for form, then form for mere number. It would have us reject those intimations of high and half-remembered things which a new aspect of a tree or house or of a landscape arouses in us. It would compel us to forget, or to let grow stale, the pleasure with which the scent of woods blest us in early youth. Perpetually this evil habit of the mind would flatten the diversity of our lives, suck out the sap of experience, kill humour and exhaust the living spring. It whispers to us the falsehood that years in their advance leave us in some way less alive, it adds to the burden upon our shoulders, not a true weight of sad knowledge as life, however well lived, must properly do, but a useless drag of despair. It would make us numb. In the field of letters it would persuade us that all things may be read and known and that nothing is worth the reading or the knowing, and that the loveliest rhythms or the most subtle connotations of words are but tricks to be despised. In the field of experience it would convince us that nothing bears a fruit and that human life is no more than anarchy or at best an unexplained fragment. Even in that highest of fields, the field of service, it would persuade us that there is nothing to serve. And if we are convinced of that, then every faculty in us turns inward and becomes useless: may be called abortive and fails its end.

These thoughts arose in me as I watched to-day from the platform of my Mill the advance of a great storm cloud; for in the majestic progress which lifted itself into the sky and marched against the north from the Channel I perceived that which the evil, modern, drying habit of thought would neglect and would attempt to make material, and also that which I very well knew was in its awfulness allied to the life of the soul.

For very many days the intense heat had

parched the Weald. The leaves dropped upon the ash and the oak, the grass was brown, our wells had failed. The little river of the clay was no more than several stagnant pools. We thought the fruits would wither; and our houses, not built for such droughts and such an ardent sun, were like ovens long after the cool of the evening had come.

At the end of some days one bank of cloud and then another had passed far off east or far to the west, over the distant forest ridge or over Egdean Side, missing us. We had printed stuff from London telling us how it had rained in London—as though rain falling in London ever fell upon earth or nourished fruits and men!

We thought that we were not to be allowed any little rain out of Heaven. But to-day the great storm came up, marching in a dark breastplate and in skirts of rain, with thunders about it; and it was personal. It came right up out of the sea. It walked through the gate which the River Adur has pierced, leaving upon either side the high chalk hills; the crest of its helmet carried a great plume of white and menacing cloud.

No man seeing this creature as it moved solemn and panoplied could have mistaken the memory or the knowledge that stirred within him at the sight. This was that great master, that great friend, that great enemy, that great idol (for it has been all of these things), which, since we have tilled the earth, we have watched, we have welcomed, we have combated, we have unfortunately worshipped. This was that God of the Storm which has made such tremendous music in the poets.

The Parish Church, which had seemed under the hard blue sky of the early morning a low brown thing, with its square tower of the Templars and of the Second Crusade, stood up now white, menacing, and visionary against the ink of the cloud. The many trees of the rich man's park beyond were taller, especially the elms. They stood absolutely and stubbornly still, no leaves upon them moving at all.

THE STORM

The Downs an hour away first fell dull, low, and leaden. These were but half seen, and at last faded altogether into the gloom. The many beasts round about were struck with silence. The fowls nestled together, and the only sign that animate nature gave of an approaching stroke was the whinny of a horse in a stable where the door was left wide open to the stifling air, and the mad circling and swooping of a bird distracted by the change in the light.

For the sun was now blotted out, and the enormous thing was upon us like a foe. First I saw from the high platform of my Mill a sort of driving mist or whirl, which at first I thought to be an arrow-shoot of rain; but looking again I saw it to be no more than the dust of many parched fields and lanes, driving before the edge of the thunder. There was a wind preceding all this like a herald. In a moment the oppressive air grew cool. It grew cool by a leap. It was like the descent into a cellar; it was like the opening of a mine door to a draft. The vigour of the mind, dulled by so many days of heat and nights without refreshment, leaped up to greet this change, which, though it came under a solemn and uncomforting aspect, gave breath and expansion. One might for some five minutes have imagined as the dust clouds advanced and the furious shaking of the trees and hedges a mile away began to be heard as well as seen, that the call of coolness for work had come. Then that wall of wind hit the two great oaks of my neighbour next to my own frontier trees. The fan of the Mill groaned, turning a little; it turned furiously, and the strength of the storm was upon us. It lightened, single and double and fourfold. The blinding fire sprang from arch to arch of an incredible architecture, higher than anything you might dream of, larger than the mountains of other lands. The thunder ran through all this, not very loud but continuous, and a sweep of darkness followed like a train after the movement of the cloud. White wreaths blown out in jets as though by some caprice in wilful shapes showed here and there, and here and there, against such a blackness, grey cloudlets drifted very rapidly, hurrying distracted left and right without a purpose. All the while the rain fell.

The village and the landscape and the Weald, the Rape, the valley, all my county you would have said, was swallowed up, occupied, and overwhelmed. It was more majestic than an army; it was a victory more absolute than any achievement of arms, and while it flashed and poured and proclaimed itself with its continual noise, it was itself, as it were, the thing in which we lived, and the mere earth was but a scene upon which the great storm trod for the purpose of its pageant.

When the storm had passed over northward to other places beyond, and when at evening the stars came out very numerous and clear in a sky which the thunder had not cooled, and when the doubtful summer haze was visible again very low upon the distant horizon, over the English sea, the memory of all this was like

THE STORM

the memory of a complete achievement. No
one who had seen the storm could doubt purpose
or meaning in the vastness of things, nor the
creative word of Almighty God.

XXVIII

THE VALLEY

EVERYBODY knows, I fancy, that kind of landscape in which hills seem to lie in a regular
manner, fold on fold, one range behind the
other, until at last, behind them all, some higher
and grander range dominates and frames the
whole.

The infinite variety of light and air and
accident of soil provide all men, save those
who live in the great plains, with examples
of this sort. The traveller in the dry air of
California or of Spain, watching great dis-
tances from the heights, will recollect such
landscapes all his life. They were the reward
of his long ascents, and they were the sunset
visions which attended his effort when at last
he had climbed to the utmost ridge of his
day's westward journey. Such a landscape
does a man see from the edges of the Guadar-

rama, looking eastward and south toward the very distant hills that guard Toledo and the ravines of the Tagus. Such a landscape does a man see at sunrise from the highest of the Cevennes looking right eastward to the dawn as it comes up in the pure and cold air beyond the Alps, and shows you the falling of their foothills, a hundred miles of them, right down to the trench of the Rhone. And by such a landscape is a man gladdened when, upon the escarpments of the Tuolumne, he turns back and looks westward over the Stockton plain towards the coast range which guards the Pacific.

The experience of such a sight is one peculiar in travel, or, for that matter, if a man is lucky enough to enjoy it near his home, insistent and reiterated upon the mind of the home-dwelling man. Such a landscape, for instance, makes a man praise God if his house is upon the height of Mendip, and he can look over falling hills right over the Vale of Severn toward the rank above rank of the Welsh solemnities beyond, until the straight line and height of the Black Mountain against the sky bounds his view and frames it.

It is the character of these landscapes to suggest at once a vastness, a diversity, and a seclusion. When a man comes upon them unexpectedly he can forget the perpetual toil of men and imagine that those who dwell below in the nearer glens before him are exempt from the necessities of this world. When such a landscape is part of a man's dwelling place, though he well knows that the painful life of men within those hills is the same hard business that it is throughout the world, yet his knowledge is modified and comforted by the permanent glory of the thing he sees.

The distant and high range that bounds his view makes a sort of wall, cutting the country off and guarding it from whatever may be beyond. The succession of lower ranges suggests secluded valleys, and the reiterated woods, distant and more distant, convey an impression of fertility more powerful than that of corn in harvest upon the lowlands.

THE VALLEY

Sometimes it is a whole province that is thus grasped by the eye; sometimes in the summer haze of Northern lands, a few miles only; always this scenery inspires the onlooker with a sense of completion and of repose, and at the same time, I think, with worship and with awe.

Now one such group of valleys there was, hill above hill, forest above forest, and beyond it a great, noble range, unwooded and high against Heaven, guarding all the place, which I for my part knew from the day when first I came to know anything of this world. There is a high place under fir trees; a place of sand and bracken in South England, whence such a view was always present to my eye in childhood, and "There," said I to myself (even in childhood) "a man should make his habitation. In those valleys is the proper settling place for a man."

And so there was. There was a steading for me in the midst of those hills.

It was a little place which had grown up

as my county grows, the house throwing out
arms and layers, and making itself over ten
generations of men. One room was panelled
in the oak of the seventeenth century—but that
had been a novelty in its time, for the walls
upon which the panels stood were of the late
fifteenth, oak and brick intermingled. Another
room was large and light, built in the manner
of one hundred and fifty years ago, which
people call Georgian.

It had been thrown out South—and this
is quite against our custom; for our older
houses looked east and west to take all the
sun and to present a corner to the south-west
and the storms. So they stand still.

It had round it a solid cornice which the
modern men of the towns would have called
ugly, but there was ancestry in it. Then,
further on this house had modern roominess
stretching in one new wing after another;
and it had a great set of byres and barns,
and there was a copse and some six acres of
land. Over a deep gully stood over against

it the little town that was the mother of the place; and altogether this good place was enclosed, silent, and secure.

" The fish that misses the hook regrets the worm." If this is not a Chinese proverb it ought to be. That little farm and steading and those six acres, that ravine, those trees, that aspect of the little mothering town; the wooded hills fold above fold, the noble range beyond—all these were not, and for ever will not be mine.

For all I know some man quite unacquainted with that land took the place, grumbling, for a debt; or again, for all I know it may have been bought by a blind man who could not see the hills, or by some man who, seeing them perpetually, regretted the flat marshes of his home. To-day, this very day, up high on Egdean Side, not thinking of such things, through a gap in the trees, I saw again after so many years, set one behind the other, the woods, wave upon wave, the summer heat, the high, bare range guarding all; and in the midst of that landscape, set like a toy, the little Sabine farm.

Then, said I, to this place I might not know, " Continue. Go and serve whom you will. You were not altogether mine because you would not be, and to-day you are not mine at all. You will regret it perhaps, and perhaps you will not. There was verse in you perhaps, or prose, or, much better still (for all I know), contentment for a man. But you refused. You lost your chance. Good-by," and with that I went on into the wood and beyond the gap and saw the sight no more.

It was ten years since I had seen it last, the little Sabine farm. It may be ten years before I see it again, or it may be for ever. But as I went through the woods saying to myself:

" You lost your chance, my little Sabine farm, you lost your chance ! " another part of me at once replied:

" Ah, and so did you ! "

Then, by way of riposte, I answered in my
mind:

"Not at all, for the chance I never had;
all I have lost is my desire—no more."

"No, not only your desire," said the voice
to me within, "but the fulfilment of it." And
when that reply came I naturally turned, as
all men do on hearing such interior replies, to
a general consideration of regret, and was prepared, if any honest publisher should have
come whistling through that wood, with an
offer proper to the occasion to produce no less
than five volumes on the Nature of Regret, its
mortal sting, its bitter-sweetness, its power to
keep alive in man the pure passions of the
soul, its hint at immortality, its memory of
Heaven.

But the wood was empty. The offer did not
come. The moment was lost. The five volumes will hardly now be written. In place of
them I offer poor this, which you may take or
leave. But I beg leave, before I end, to cite
certain words very nobly attached to that great

THE VALLEY

inn, The Griffin, which has its foundation set
far off in another place, in the town of March,
in the sad Fen-Land near the Eastern Sea:

"England my desire, what have you not refused?"

XXIX

A CONVERSATION IN ANDORRA

THE other day—indeed some months ago—I was in the company of two men who were talking together and were at cross-purposes. The one was an Englishman acquainted with the Catalonian tongue and rather proud of knowing it; the other was a citizen of the Republic of Andorra.

The first had the advantage of his fellow in world-wide travel, the reading of many newspapers and (beside his thorough knowledge of Catalonian) a smattering of French, German, and American.

I was touched to see the care and deference and good-fellowship which the superior extended to the inferior in this colloquy.

I did not hear the beginning of it: it was the early middle part which I came in for; it was conducted loudly and with gestures upon the part of the Andorran, good-humouredly but equally openly on the part of the Englishman, who said:

" I grant you that life is very hard for some of our town dwellers in spite of the high wages they obtain."

To which the Andorran answered: " There is nothing to grant, your Grace, for I would not believe their life was hard; but I was puzzled by what you told me, for I could not make out how they earned so much money, and yet looked so extraordinary." The Andorran showed by this that he had visited England.

At this the Englishman smiled pleasantly enough and said: " Do you think me extraordinary? "

The Andorran was a little embarrassed. " No no," he said, " you do not understand the word I use. I do not mean extraordinary to see, I mean unhappy and lacking humanity."

The Englishman smiled more genially still

in his good wholesome beard, and said: " Do
I look to you like that? "

" No," said the Andorran gravely, " nor
does that gentleman whom you pointed out
to me when we left France, your English
patron, Mr. Bernstein I think . . . you were
both well-fed and well-clothed . . . and what
is more, I know nothing of what you earn.
But in Andorra we ask about this man and
that man indifferently, and especially about
the poorest, and when I asked you about the
poorest in your towns you told me that there
was not one of them who did not earn, when
he was fully working, twenty-five pesetas a
week. Now with twenty-five pesetas a week!
Oh . . .! Why, I could live on five, and five
weeks of twenty saved is a hundred pesetas; and
with a hundred pesetas . . .! Oh, one can buy
a great brood sow; or if one is minded for
grandeur, the best coat in the world; or again,
a little mule just foaled, which in two years,
mind you, *in two years* " (and here he wagged
his finger) " will be a great fine beast " (and

here he extended his arms), "and the *next* year will carry a man over the hills and will sell for five hundred pesetas. Yes it will!"

The Englishman looked puzzled. "Well," said he, leaning forward, ticking off on his fingers and becoming practical, "there's your pound a week."

The Andorran nodded. He began ticking it off on his fingers also.

"Now of course the man is not always in work."

"If he is lazy," said the Andorran with angry eyes, "the neighbours shall see to that!"

"No," said the Englishman, irritated, "you don't understand; he can't always find some one to *give* him work."

"But who *gives* work?" said the Andorran. "Work is not *given*." And then he laughed. "Our trouble is to get the youngsters to do it!" And he laughed more loudly.

"You don't understand," repeated the Englishman, pestered, "he can't work unless some one allows him to work for him."

" Pooh ! " said the Andorran, " he could cut down trees or dig, or get up into the hills."

" Why," said the Englishman with wondering eyes, " the perlice would have him then."

The Andorran looked mournful: he had heard the name of something dangerous in this country. He thought it was a ghost that haunted lonely places and strangled men.

" Well then," went on the Englishman in a practical fashion, again ticking on his fingers, " let us say he can work three weeks out of the five."

" Yes? " said the Andorran, bewildered.

" He gets, let us say, three times a week's wage in the five weeks. . . . I don't mind, call it an average of twenty pesetas if you like, or even eighteen."

" What is an ' average '? " said the Andorran, frowning.

" An average," said the Englishman impatiently, " oh, an average is what he gets all lumped up."

" Do you mean," said the Andorran gravely,

"that he gets eighteen pesetas every Saturday?"

"No, *no*, no!" struck in the Englishman. "Twenty-five pesetas, as you call them, when he can get work, and nothing when he can't."

"Good Lord!" said the Andorran, with wide eyes and crossing himself. "How does the poor fellow know whether perlice will not be at him again? It is enough to break a man's heart!"

"Well, don't *argue!*" said the Englishman, keen upon his tale. "He gets an average, anyhow, of eighteen pesetas, as you call them, a week. Now you see, however wretched he is, five of those will go in rent, and if he is a decent man, seven."

The Andorran was utterly at sea. "But if he is wretched, why should he pay, and if he is decent why should he pay still more?" he asked.

"Why, damn it all!" said the Englishman, exploding, "a man must live!"

"Precisely," said the Andorran rigidly, "that is why I am asking the question. He pays this tax, you say, five pesetas, if he is wretched and seven if he is decent. But a man may be decent although he is wretched, and who is so brutal as to ask a tax of the poor?"

"It isn't a tax," said the Englishman. "He pays it for his house."

"But a man could buy a house," said the Andorran, "with a few payments like that."

The Englishman sighed. "Do listen to my explanation. He's got to pay it anyhow."

"Well," said the Andorran, sighing in his turn, "you must have a wicked King. But, please God, he cannot spend it all on his pleasures."

"It isn't paid to the King, God bless him," said the Englishman. "The man pays it to his landlord."

"And suppose he doesn't?" said the Andorran defiantly.

"Well, the perlice," began the Englishman, and the Andorran's face showed that he was afraid of occult powers.

CONVERSATION IN ANDORRA

" So there, you see," went on the English-man, calculating along with rapid content, " he's only got thirteen."

The Andorran was willing to stretch a point. " Well," said he doubtfully, " I will grant him thirteen, and with thirteen pesetas a man can do well enough. His wife milks, and it does not cost much to put a little cotton on the child, and then, of course, if he is too poor to buy a bed, why there is his straw."

" Straw's not decent, and we don't allow it," said the Englishman firmly; " he doesn't buy a bed always; sometimes he rents it."

" I don't understand," said the Andorran, " I don't understand."

There was a little pause during which neither of the two men looked at the other. The Eng-lishman went on good-naturedly and laboriously explaining:

" Now let's come to bread."

" Yes," said the Andorran eagerly, " man lives by bread and wine."

" Well," said the Englishman, ignoring this

interruption, "you see, bread for the lot of them would come to half that money."

"Yes," said the Andorran, nodding, "you are quite right. Bread is a very serious thing." And he sighed.

"Half of it," continued the Englishman, "goes in bread. And then, of course, he has to get a little meat."

"Certainly," said the Andorran.

"Bacon anyhow," the Englishman went on, "and there's boots."

"Oh, he could do without boots," said the Andorran.

"No he can't," said the Englishman, "they all have to have boots; and then you see, there's tea."

The Andorran was interested in hearing about tea. "You Englishmen are so fond of tea," he said, smiling. "I have noticed that you ask for tea. Juan has tea to sell."

The Englishman nodded genially. "I will buy some of him," he said.

"Well, go on," said the Andorran.

"And there's a little baccy, of course "—
and he gave the prices of both those articles.
"They're a leetle more than you might think,"
continued the Englishman, a little confused.
"They're taxed, you see."

"Taxed again?" said the Andorran.

"Yes," said the Englishman rapidly, "not
much; besides which, I haven't said anything
was taxed yet: they pay about double on their
tea and about four times on the value of the tobacco. But they don't feel it. Oh, if they get
regular work they're all right!"

"Then," said the Andorran, summing it all
up, "they ought to do very well."

"Yes, they ought," said the Englishman,
"but somehow they're not steady of themselves:
they get *pauperised*."

"What is that?" said the Andorran.

"Why, they get to expect things for
nothing."

"They think," said the Andorran cheerfully,
"that good things fall from the sky. I know
that sort: we have them." He thought he had

begun to understand, and just after he had said this we came to a village.

I must here tell you what I ought to have put at the beginning of these few lines, that I heard this conversation in Andorra valley itself, while four of us, the Andorran guide, the Englishman, myself and an Ironist were proceeding through the mountains, riding upon mules.

We had come to the village of Encamps, and there we all got down to enter the inn. We had a meal together and paid, the four of us, exactly five shillings and threepence all together for wine and bread, cooked meat, plenty of vegetables, coffee, liqueurs and a cigar.

This was the end of the conversation in Andorra: it was my business to return to England after the holiday to write an essay on a point in political economy, to which I did justice; but the conventions of academic writing prevented me from quoting in that essay this remarkable experience.

XXX

PARIS AND THE EAST

ONE of the things that set a modern man wondering is the nature of the survivor of our time.

It is customary to say that all human things decay and end; and if you will take a period long enough of course it is true, for at last the world itself shall dissolve. But when men point to dead Empires, as Egypt or Assyria are dead, or when they point to a fossilised civilisation, as it seems, according to travellers, that certain civilisations of the East are fossilised, or when they point to little broken cities where once were famous towns, one is. tempted to remember that to all these there is an exceptional glorious sort which is ourselves. Atlantic Europe, the Europe that was made by the Christian Faith and in the first four centuries of our era, lives on from change to change in a most marvellous way, and for now two thousand years has not seemed capable of decline. You have in the history of it resurrection after resurrection, and through all those rapid and fantastic developments, transformations far more rapid and far more fantastic than any other of which we have record, a sort of inner fixity of type remains, like the individual soul of the man which makes him always himself in spite of accident and in spite of the process of age; only, Europe differs from such metaphor in this, that it is like some man not subject, it would seem, to mortality.

This thought to which I perpetually return, occurred to me as I handled a book on Paris, the illustrations of which were impressions gathered by a Japanese artist. Such a contrast will call up in the minds of many the contrast between something very old and something very new. A reader might say as he glanced at this book: " Here is one of the most ancient things we have, the Oriental mind, and it is looking at one of the freshest and most modern things we have, modern Paris."

I confess that to me the contrast is of another kind. I should say: " Here is something which is, so far as its inner force goes, immovable, the Oriental mind; and this is how it looks at the most mobile thing on earth, the heart of Gaul—yet the mobile thing has a history almost as long as, and far more full than, the immobile thing."

Upon a central page of this book I found a really splendid bit of drawing. It is an impression of the Statue of the Republic under a cold dawn. Now when one thinks what that statue means, what portion of the stoical philosophy re-arisen after so many centuries it embodies, what furious combats have raged round that idea: I mean combats, not debates: pain, not rhetoric; men dying in great numbers and desiring to kill others as they died. When one considers that statue but the other day, with the raging mob of workmen round it, and when one suddenly remembers that the whole thing is after all only of the last hundred years—what a multiplicity of life this chief of our European cities possesses in one's eyes!

The admirable pictures in this book are drawn as nearly in the European manner as one could expect, but the feeling is an unchanging feeling which we know in Eastern things. The mind is like deep and level water, never stirred by wind: a big lake in a crater of the hills. But the thing drawn is as moving and as living as the air.

I wonder whether this artist, as he stood and drew, felt as a European feels when he stands and draws in any one of our immemorial sites: by the Pool of London, or at the top of the rue St. Jacques, or in the place of the Martyrdom at Toulouse, or looking at the most ancient yellow dusts of Toledo from over the tumbling strength of the Tagus? He may have felt it . . . perhaps . . . for all his work, even the little introduction that he has written shows that astonishing adaptability and exceedingly rapid intelligence which are the marks of the Japanese to-day. But if he felt it he must have felt it by education. For us it is in our blood. We stand upon those sites and we feel ourself in and part of a stream of life that seems almost incapable of ending. And that brings me back to where I began, How much longer will our civilisation endure?

Will it end? It has many enemies, most of them unconscious, has modern Europe.

It has men within it who imagine that the correction of some large abuse and the withdrawal of some considerable part of its fabric in the correction of that abuse, is a matter concerning only their one generation. These men visibly put in peril the balance of that civilisation by their very enthusiasm.

It has a lesser number of other enemies within itself; enemies more dangerous, who do believe that some quite new thing wholly alien to the soul of Europe can be imposed upon that soul. These men are always for anarchy; they delight in emphasising all that seems to diminish the responsibility and the freedom of citizens, and it is their pleasure to accelerate every tendency which may destroy, from whatever side, our permanent solution of domestic and of natural things: families, properties, armies.

The common faith which was, as it were, the cement of our civilisation has been hit so hard that some do ask themselves openly the question that was only whispered some little time ago—whether the cement still holds. It is quite certain that if that last symbol and reality disintegrates, if the Catholic Church leaves it, Europe has come to an end.

But these questions are not yet to be met by any reply. And when I ask myself those questions, and I always do when I see the Seine going by the walls that were Cæsar's parleying ground with the chiefs, Dionysius's prison, Julian's office, Dagobert's palace, and which have been subject to everything from Charlemagne to the Bourbons, and which have (within the memory of men whom I myself have known) ended the Monarchy and seen passing by a wholly new society—when I ask myself those questions, I answer less and less with every year.

Time was, in the University, say twenty years ago, one would have said: "It is all over. Everything that can destroy us has triumphed." Time was, say ten years ago, in the heat of a particular struggle which raged all over the West, one could have said with the enthusiasm of the fight, that continuity would win. But to-day, whether because one has accumulated knowledge or because things are really more confused, it is difficult to reply.

.   .   .   .   .

A man with our knowledge and our experience of what Europe has been and is, standing in the grey and decayed Roman city of the Fifth Century, and watching the little barbarian troop riding into Lutetia, might have said that a gradual darkness would swallow us all, especially since he knew that just beyond the narrow seas in Eastern Britain a dense pall then covered the corpse of the Roman civilisation.

A man working on the Tour St. Jacques, the

last of the Gothic, might have seen nothing but anarchy and the end of all good work in the change that was surging round him: the Huguenots, the new Splendour, the cruelty and the making of lies.

Certainly those who were present in Paris *before* the 10th of August, '92, thought an end had come, and believed the Revolution to be a most unfruitful and tempestuous death; imagining Europe to have no hope but in the possible extinction of the flame.

All three judgments would have been wrong. And when one takes that typical Paris again, and handles it and looks at it and thinks of it as the example and the symbol of all our time; just as one is beginning to say " The thing is dying," the memory of similar deaths that were not deaths in the past returns to one and one must be silent.

Never was Europe less conscious of herself, never did she more freely admit the forces that destroy, than she admits them to-day. Never was evil more insolently or more glaringly in power; never had it less fear of chastisement than in the whirlwind of our time. If that whirlwind is mechanical, and if this vast anarchic commerce, these blaring papers, these sudden fortunes, these frequent and unparalleled huge wars, are the breaking up of all that once made Europe, then the answer to the question is plain: but it may be that these are things not mechanical but organic: seeds surviving in the ruin which will grow up into living forms. We shall see.

XXXI

THE HUMAN CHARLATAN

IT is curious that the Scientific Spirit has never tabulated any research, even superficial, upon the human type of charlatan.

It is the essence of a charlatan that he aims at the results of certain excellences in the full consciousness that he does not possess those excellences. The material upon which he works is twofold: the ignorance and the noble appetite for reverence in his fellow men.

Where animals are concerned the Scientific Spirit has tabulated a good deal of careful research in this department. We know fairly well the habits of the Cuckoo. What seemingly harmless organisms are poisonous to us, and why, we have discovered and can catalogue. The successful deception practised for purposes of secrecy or greed by such and such a creature, we can discover in our books. But no one has tabulated the human charlatan.

An admirable example upon which one can test the whole theory of charlatanism is the ridiculous Lombroso.

To begin with you have the name. He was no more of an Italian than Disraeli, or than the present Mayor of Rome: but his Italian name deceives and is intended to deceive, not necessarily that it was assumed, but that it was paraded as national. Hundreds of honest men thought themselves praising the Italian character and Italian civilisation when the newspapers (themselves half duped) had persuaded them to blow the trumpet of Lombroso.

One of the characteristics of the charlatan is that he parades the object with which he desires to dupe you, and simultaneously hides his methods in pushing the thing forward. The purveyor of cheap jewellery in Whitechapel does this. He lets you have the glitter of his article full and strong. Where he got it, of his own connection with it, and what it is, you learn last in the business or not at all. The whole process is one of suggestion, or, as our forefathers called it, " hoodwinking." Lombroso was true to type in this regard.

The European Press was deluged one day with notices, praise, reviews of a book which was called *Degeneration.* It was a tenth-rate book, but we were compelled to hear of it. No words were fine enough to describe its author. We learnt that his name was Nordau. There was no process of logic in the book, there was no labour. Where it asserted (it was a mass of assertions) it usually trespassed on ground which the author could not pretend to any familiarity with. Those who are already alive to the international trick were suspicious and upon their guard from the very moment that they smelt the thing. The infinitely larger number who do not understand the nature of international forces were taken in. For one man who read the farrago a hundred were taught to magnify the name of Nordau. Only when this process of suggestion had well sunk in did the

THE HUMAN CHARLATAN

public casually learn that the said Nordau was a connection of Lombroso's.

A book of greater value (which is not saying much) proceeded from the pen of one Ferrero. It proposed an examination of the Roman Empire and the Roman people. Its thesis was, of course, a degradation of both. For one man who so much as saw that book, a hundred went away with the vague impression that a certain great Ferrero dominated European thought. He gave opinions (among other things) upon the polity of England so absurd and ignorant that, had the process of suggestion not run on before, those opinions would only have attained some small measure of notoriety from their very fatuousness. But the international trick had reversed the common and healthy process of human thought. We were not allowed to judge the man by his work; no, we must accept the work on the authority of the man; only after the trick had been successfully worked did it come out that Ferrero was a connection of Lombroso's.

THE HUMAN CHARLATAN

Lombroso's own department of charlatanry was to attack Christian morals in the shape of denying man's power of choice between good and evil.

In another epoch and with other human material to work upon his stock-in-trade would have taken some other form, but Lombroso had been born into that generation immediately preceding our own, whose chief intellectual vice was materialism. A name could be cheaply made upon the lines of materialism, and Lombroso took to it as naturally as his spiritual forerunners took to rationalist Deism and as his spiritual descendants will take to spurious mysticism. We shall have in the near future our Lombrosos of the Turning Table, the Rapping Devil, and the Manifesting Dead Great Aunt—indeed this development coincided with his own old age— but as things were, the easiest charlantry in his years of vigour was to be pursued upon Materialist lines, and on Materialist lines did the worthy Lombroso proceed. His method was childishly simple, and we ought to blush for our time or rather for that of our immediate seniors that it should have duped anybody—but it was far from childishly guileless.

When the laws are chiefly concerned in defending the possessions of those already wealthy, and when society, in the decline or depression of religion, takes to the worshipping of wealth, those whom the laws will punish are generally poor. Such a time was that into which Lombroso was born. No man was executed for treason, few men were imprisoned for it. Cheating on a large scale was an avenue to social advancement in most of the progressive European countries. The purveying of false news was a way to fortune: the forestaller and the briber were masters of the Senate. The sword was sheathed. The popular instinct which would repress and punish cowardice, oppression, the sexual abominations of the rich, and their cruelties, had no outlet for its expression. The prisons of Europe were filled in the main with the least responsible, the weakest willed, and the most unfortunate of the very poor. We owe to Lombroso the epoch-making discovery that the weakest willed, the least responsible, and the most unfortunate of the very poor often suffer from physical degradation. With such an intellectual equipment Lombroso erected the majestic structure of human irresponsibility.

Two hundred men and women are arrested for picking pockets in such and such a district in the course of a year. The contempt for human dignity which is characteristic of modern injustice permits these poor devils to be treated like so many animals, to be thrashed, tortured, caged, and stripped: measured, recorded, dealt with as vile bodies for experiment. Lombroso (or for that matter any one possessed of a glimmering of human reason) can see that of these two hundred unfortunate wretches, a larger proportion will be diseased or malformed, than would be the case among two hundred taken at random among the better fed or better housed and more carefully nurtured citizens. The Charlatan is in clover! He gathers his

268

statistics: twenty-three per cent. squint, eighteen per cent. have lice—what is really *conclusive* no less than ninety-three per cent. suffer from metagrobolisation of the hyperdromedaries, which is scientist Greek for the consequences of not having enough to eat. It does not take much knowledge of men and things to see what the Charlatan can make of such statistics. Lombroso pumps the method dry and then produces a theory uncommonly comfortable to the well-to-do—that their fellow-men if unfortunate can be treated as irresponsible chattels.

There is the beginning and end of the whole humbug.

With the characteristic lack of reason which is at once the weakness and the strength of this vicious clap-trap, a totally disconnected—and equally obvious—series of facts is dragged in. If men drink too much, or if they have inherited insanity, or are in any other way afflicted, by their own fault or that of others, in the action of the will, they will be prone to irresponsibilities and to follies; and where such irresponsibilities and follies endanger the comfort of the well-to-do, the forces of modern society will be used to restrain them. Their acts of violence or of unrestrained cupidity being unaccompanied by calculation will lead to the lock-up. And so you have another stream of statistics showing that " alcoholism " (which is Scientist for drinking too much) and epilepsy and lunacy do not make for material success.

On these two disparate legs poses the rickety structure which has probably already done its worst in European jurisprudence and against which the common sense of society is already reacting.

Fortunately for men Charlatanry of that calibre has no very permanent effect. It is too silly and too easily found out. If Lombroso had for one moment intended a complete theory of Materialist morals or had for one moment believed in the stuff which he used for self-advertisement, he would have told us how physically to distinguish the cosmopolitan and treasonable financier, the fraudulent company-worker, the traitor, the tyrant, the pornographer, and the coward. These in high places are the curse of modern Europe—not the most wretched of the very poor. Of course Lombroso could tell us nothing of the sort; for there is nothing to tell.

Incidentally it is worthy of remark that this man was one of those charlatans who are found out in time. Common sense revolted and in revolting managed to expose its enemy very effectively while that enemy was still alive. A hundred tricks were played upon the fellow: it is sufficient to quote two.

After a peculiarly repulsive trial for murder in Paris, a wag sent the photograph of two hands, a right hand and a left hand, to the great criminologist, telling him they were those of the murderer, and asking for his opinion. He replied in a document crammed with the pompous terms of the scientific cheap-jack, hybrid Greek and Latin, and barbarous in the extreme. He discovered malformations in the fingers and twenty other mysteries of his craft, which exactly proved why these hands were necessarily and by the predestination of blind Nature the hands of a murderer. Then it was that the wag published his letter and the reply with the grave annotation that the left hand was his own (he was a man of letters) and the right hand that of an honest fellow who washed down his carriage.

The other anecdote is as follows: Lombroso produced a piece of fatuous nonsense about the Political Criminal Woman. He based it upon " the skull of Charlotte Corday "—which skull he duly analysed, measured, and labelled with the usual regiment of long and incomprehensible words. Upon the first examination of the evidence it turned out that the skull was no more Charlotte Corday's than Queen Anne's—a medical student had sold it to a humble Curiosity Shop, and the dealer, who seems to have had some intellectual affinity with the Lombroso tribe, had labelled it for purposes of sale, " The Skull of Charlotte Corday." Lombroso swallowed it.

The Ass!

XXXII

THE BARBARIANS

The use of analogy, which is so wise and necessary a thing in historical judgment, has a knack of slipping into the falsest forms.

When ancient civilisation broke down its breakdown was accompanied by the infiltration of barbaric auxiliaries into the Roman armies, by the settlement of Barbarians (probably in small numbers), upon Roman land, and, in some provinces, by devastating, though not usually permanent, irruptions of barbaric hordes.

The presence of these foreign elements, coupled with the gradual loss of so many arts, led men to speak of " the Barbarian invasions " as though these were a principal cause of what was in reality no more than the old age and fatigue of an antique society.

Upon the model of this conception men, watching the dissolution of our own civilisation

273

to-day, or at least its corruption, have asked themselves whence those Barbarians would come that should complete its final ruin. The first, the least scholarly and the most obvious idea was that of the swamping of Europe by the East. It was a conception which required no learning, nor even any humour. It was widely adopted and it was ridiculous. Others, with somewhat more grasp of reality, coined the phrase " that the barbarians which should destroy the civilisation of Europe were already breeding under the terrible conditions of our great cities." This guess contained, indeed, a half-truth, for though the degradation of human life in the great industrial cities of England and the United States was not a cause of our decline it was very certainly a symptom of it. Moreover, industrial society, notably in this country and in Germany, while increasing rapidly in numbers, is breeding steadily from the worst and most degraded types.

But the truth is that no such mechanical explanation will suffice to set forth the causes of a civilisation's decay. Before the barbarian in any form can appear in it, it must already have weakened. If it cannot absorb or reject an alien element it is because its organism has grown enfeebled, and its powers of digestion and excretion are lost or deteriorated; and whoever would restore any society which menaces to fall, must busy himself about the inward nature of that society much more than about its external dangers or the merely mechanical and numerical factors of peril to be discovered within it.

Whenever we look for " the barbarian," whether in the decline of our own society or that of some past one whose historical fate we may be studying, we are looking rather for a visible effect of disease than for its source.

None the less to mark those visible effects is instructive, and without some conspectus of them it will be impossible to diagnose the disease. A modern man may, therefore, well ask where the barbarians are that shall enter into our inheritance, or whose triumphs shall, if it be permitted, at least accompany, even if they cannot effect, the destruction of Christendom.

With that word " Christendom " a chief part of the curious speculation is at once suggested. Whether the scholar hates or loves, rejects or adopts, ridicules or admires, the religious creed of Europe, he must, in any case, recognise two prime historical truths. The first is that that creed which we call the Christian religion was the soul and meaning of European civilisation during the period of its active and united existence. The second is that wherever the religion characteristic of a people has failed to react against its own decay and has in some last catastrophe perished, then that people has lost soon after its corporate existence.

So much has passion taken the place of reason in matters of scholarship that plain truths of this kind, to which all history bears witness, are accepted or rejected rather by the appetite of the reader than by his rational recognition of them, or his rational disagreement. If we will forget for a moment what we may *desire* in the

matter and merely consider what we *know*, we
shall without hesitation admit both the proposi-
tions I have laid down. Christendom was Christian, not by accident or superficially, but in a
formative connection, just as an Englishman is
English or as a poem is informed by a definite
scheme of rhythm. It is equally true that a
sign and probably a cause of a society's end is
the dissolution of that causative moral thing, its
philosophy or creed.

Now here we discover the first mark of the
Barbarian.

Note that in the peril of English society to-
day there is no positive alternative to the ancient philosophic tradition of Christian Europe.
It has to meet nothing more substantive than a
series of negations, often contradictory, but
all allied in their repugnance to a fixed certitude
in morals.

So far has this process gone that to be writing as I am here in public, not even defending
the creed of Christendom, but postulating its
historic place, and pointing out that the con-

siderable attack now carried on against it is symptomatic of the dissolution of our society, has about it something temerarious and odd.

Next look at secondary effects and consider how certain root institutions native to the long development of Europe and to her individuality are the subject of attack and note the nature of the attack.

A fool will maintain that change, which is the law of life, can be presented merely as a matter of degree, and that, because our institutions have always been subject to change, therefore their very disappearance can proceed without the loss of all that has in the past been ourselves.

But an argument of this sort has no weight with the serious observer. It is certain that if the fundamental institutions of a polity are no longer regarded as fundamental by its citizens, that polity is about to pass through the total change which in a living organism we call death.

THE BARBARIANS

Now the modern attack upon property and upon marriage (to take but two fundamental institutions of the European) is precisely of this nature. Our peril is not that certain men attack the one or the other and deny their moral right to exist. Our peril rather is that, quite as much as those who attack, those who defend seem to take for granted the relativeness, the artificiality, the non-fundamental character of the institution which they are apparently concerned to support.

See how marriage is defended. To those who would destroy it under the plea of its inconveniences and tragedies, the answer is no longer made that, good or ill, it is an absolute and is intangible. The answer made is that it is convenient, or useful, or necessary, or merely traditional.

Most significant of all, the terminology of the attack is on the lips of the defence, but the contrary is never the case. Those opponents of marriage who abound in modern England will never use the term " a sacrament," yet how many for whom marriage is still a sacrament will forego the pseudo-scientific jargon of their opponents?

The threat against property is upon the same lines. That property should be restored that most citizens should enjoy it, that it is normal to the European family in its healthy state—all this we hear less and less. More and more do we hear it defended, however morbid in form or unjust in use, as a necessity, a trick which secures a greater stability for the State or a mere power which threatens and will break its opponents tyrannously.

The spirit is abroad in many another minor matter. In its most grotesque form it challenges the accuracy of mathematics: in its most vicious, the clear processes of the human reason. The Barbarian is as proud as a savage in a top hat when he talks of the elliptical or the hyperbolic universe and tries to picture parallel straight lines converging or diverging—but never doing anything so vulgarly old-fashioned as to remain parallel.

THE BARBARIANS

The Barbarian when he has graduated to be a " pragmatist," struts like a nigger in evening clothes, and believes himself superior to the gift of reason, or free to maintain that definition, limit, quantity and contradiction are little childish things which he has outgrown.

The Barbarian is very certain that the exact reproduction in line or colour of a thing seen is beneath him, and that a drunken blur for line, a green sky, a red tree and a purple cow for colour, are the mark of great painting.

The Barbarian hopes—and that is the very mark of him—that he can have his cake and eat it too. He will consume what civilisation has slowly produced after generations of selection and effort but he will not be at the pains to replace such goods nor indeed has he a comprehension of the virtue that has brought them into being. Discipline seems to him irrational, on which account he is for ever marvelling that civilisation should have offended him with priests and soldiers.

The Barbarian wonders what strange meaning may lurk in that ancient and solemn truth, " *Sine Auctoritate nulla vita.*"

In a word, the Barbarian is discoverable everywhere in this that he cannot *make;* that he can befog or destroy, but that he cannot sustain; and of every Barbarian in the decline or peril of every civilisation exactly that has been true.

We sit by and watch the Barbarian, we tolerate him; in the long stretches of peace we are not afraid.

We are tickled by his irreverence, his comic inversion of our old certitudes and our fixed creeds refreshes us: we laugh. But as we laugh we are watched by large and awful faces from beyond: and on these faces there is no smile.

We permit our jaded intellects to play with drugs of novelty for the fresh sensation they arouse, though we know well there is no good in them, but only wasting at the last.

Yet there is one real interest in watching the Barbarian and one that is profitable.

The real interest of watching the Barbarian

is not the amusement derivable from his antics, but the prime doubt whether he will succeed or no, whether he will flourish. He is, I repeat, not an agent, but merely a symptom, yet he should be watched as a symptom. It is not he in his impotence that can discover the power to disintegrate the great and ancient body of Christendom, but if we come to see him triumphant we may be certain that that body, from causes much vaster than such as he could control, is furnishing him with sustenance and forming for him a congenial soil—and that is as much as to say that we are dying.

XXXIII

ON KNOWING THE PAST

An apprehension of the past demands two kinds of information.

First, the mind must grasp the nature of historic change and must be made acquainted with the conditions of human thought in each successive period, as also with the general aspect of its revolution and progression.

Secondly, the actions of men, the times, that is the dates and hours of such actions, must be strictly and accurately acquired.

Neither of these two foundations upon which repose both the teaching and the learning of history is more important than the other. Each is essential. But a neglect of the due emphasis which one or the other demands, though both be present, warps the judgment of the scholar and forbids him to apply this science to its end, which is the establishment of truth.

ON KNOWING THE PAST

History may be called the test of true philosophy, or it may be called in a very modern and not very dignified metaphor, the object lesson of political science; or it may be called the great story whose interest is upon another plane from all other stories because its irony, its tragedy and its moral are real, were acted by real men, and were the manifestation of God.

But whatever brief and epigrammatic summary we make to explain the value of history to men, that formula still remains an imperative formula for them all, and I repeat it: the end of history is the establishment of truth.

A man may be ever so accurately informed as to the dates, the hours, the weather, the gestures, the type of speech, the very words, the soil, the colour, that between them all would seem to build up a particular event. But if he is not seized of the mind which lay behind all that was human in the business, then no synthesis of his detailed knowledge is possible. He cannot give to the various actions which he knows their due sequence and proportion; he knows not what to omit, nor what to enlarge upon, among so many, or rather a potentially infinite number of facts, and his picture will not be (as some would put it) distorted: it will be false. He will not be able to use history for its end, which is the establishment of truth. All that he establishes by his action, all that he confirms and makes stronger, is untruth. And so far as truth is concerned, it would be far better that a man should be possessed of no history than that he should be possessed of history ill-stated as to the factor of human motive.

A living man has to aid his judgment and to guide him in the establishment of truth, contemporary experience. Other men are his daily companions. The consequence and the living principles of their acts and of his own are fully within his grasp.

If a man is rightly informed of all the past motive and determining mind from which the present has sprung, his information will illumine and expand and confirm his use of that present experience. If he know nothing of the past his personal observation and the testimony of his own senses are, so far as they go, an unshakable foundation. But if he brings in aid of contemporary experience an appreciation of the past which is false because it gives to the past a mind which was not its own, then he will not only be wrong upon that past, but he will tend to be wrong also in his conclusions upon the present. He will for ever read into the plain facts before him origins and predetermining forces which do not explain them and which are not connected with them in the way he imagines. And he will easily come to regard his own society, which as a wholly uninstructed man he might fairly though insufficiently have grasped, through a veil of illusion and of false philosophy, until at last he cannot even see the things before his eyes. In a word, it is better to have no history at all than to have history which misconceives the general direction and the large lines of thought in the immediate and the remote past.

ON KNOWING THE PAST

This being evidently the case one is tempted
to say that a just estimate of the revolution and
the progression of human motive in the past is
everything to history, and that an accurate
scholarship in the details of the chronicle, in
dates especially, is of wholly inferior importance. Such a statement would be quite false.
Scholarship in history, that is an acquaintance
with the largest possible number of facts, and
an accurate retention of them in the memory,
is as essential to this study as of that other
background of motive which has just been ex-
amined.

The thing is self-evident if we put an extreme case. For if a man were wholly ignorant
of the facts of history and of their sequence, he
could not possibly know what might lie behind
the actions of the past, for we only obtain communion with that which is within and that which
is foundational in human action by an observation of its external effect.

A man's history, for instance, is sound and
on the right lines if he have but a vague and

general sentiment of the old Pagan civilisation
of the Mediterranean so long as that sentiment
corresponds to the very large outline and is in
sympathy with the main spirit of the affair.
But he cannot possess so much as an impression
of the truth if he has not heard the names of
certain of the great actors, if he is wholly unacquainted with the conception of a City State,
and if the names of Rome, of Athens, of Anti-
och, of Alexandria, and of Jerusalem have never
been mentioned to him.

Nor will a knowledge of facts, however slight,
be valuable; contrariwise it will be detrimental
and of negative value to his judgment if accuracy in his knowledge be lacking. If he were
invariably inaccurate, thinking that red which
was blue, inverting the order of any two events
and putting without fail in the summer what
happened in winter, or in the Germanies what
took place in Gaul, his facts would never corre-
spond with the human motive of them, and his
errors upon externals would at once close his
avenues of access towards internal motive and

suggest other and non-existent motive in its place.

It is, of course, a childish error to imagine that the knowledge of a time grows out of a mere accumulation of observation. External things do not produce ideas, they only reveal them. And to imagine that mere scholarship is sufficient to history is to put one's self on a level with those who, in the sphere of politics, for instance, ignore the necessity of political theory and talk muddily of the " working " of institutions—as though it were possible to judge whether an institution were working ill or not when one had no ideal that institutions might be designed to attain. But though scholarship is not the source of judgment in history, it is the invariable and the necessary accompaniment of it. Facts, which (to repeat) do not produce ideas but only reveal or suggest them, do none the less reveal and suggest them, and form the only instrument of such suggestion and revelation.

Scholarship, accurate and widespread, has

this further function: that it lends stuff to general apprehension of the past, which, however just, is the firmer, the larger and the more intense as the range of knowledge and its fixity increase. And scholarship has one more function, which is that it connects, and it connects with more and more precision in proportion as it is more and more detailed, the tendency of the mind to develop a general and perhaps justly apprehended idea into imaginary regions: for the mind is creative; it will still make and spin, and if you do not feed it with material it will spin dreams out of emptiness.

Thus a man will have a just appreciation of the thirteenth century in England; he will perhaps admire or will perhaps be repelled by its whole spirit according to his temperament or his acquired philosophy; but in either case, though his general impression was just, he will tend to add to it excrescences of judgment which, as the process continued, would at last destroy the true image were not scholarship there to come in perpetually and check him in his conclusions.

He admires it, he will tend to make it more national than it was, to forget its cruelties because what is good in our own age is not accompanied by cruelty. He will tend to lend it a science it did not possess because physical science is in our own time an accompaniment of greatness. But if he reads and reads continually, these vagaries will not oppress or warp his vision. More and more body will be added to that spirit, which he does justly but only vaguely know. And he will at last have with the English thirteenth century something of that acquaintance which one has with a human face and voice: these also are external things, and these also are the product of a soul.

Indeed—though metaphors are dangerous in such a matter—a metaphor may with reservation be used to describe the effect of the chronicle, of research and of accurate scholarship in the science of history. A man ill provided with such material is like one who sees a friend at a distance; a man well provided with it is like a man who sees a friend close at hand. Both are

certain of the identity of the person seen, both
are well founded in that certitude; but there are
errors possible to the first which are not possible to the second, and close and intimate acquaintance lends to every part of judgment a
surety which distant and general acquaintance
wholly lacks. The one can say something true
and say it briefly: there is no more to say.
The other can fill in and fill in the picture, until
though perhaps never complete, it is a symp-
totic to completion.

To increase one's knowledge by research, to
train one's self to an accurate memory of it,
does not mean that one's view of the past is continually changing. Only a fool can think, for
instance, that some document somewhere will be
discovered to show that the mass of the people
of London had for James II an ardent venera-
tion, or that the national defence organised by
the Committee of Public Safety during the
French Revolution was due to the unpopular
tyranny of a secret society. But research in
either of these cases, and a minute and in-

creasing acquaintance with detail, does show one London largely apathetic in the first place, and does show one large sections of rebellious feeling in the armies of the Terror. It permits one to appreciate what energy and what initiative were needed for the overthrow of the Stuarts, and to see from how small a body of wealthy and determined men that policy proceeded. It permits one to understand how the battles of '93 could never have been fought upon the basis of popular enthusiasm alone; it permits one to assert without exaggeration that the autocratic power of the Committee of Public Safety and the secrecy of its action was a necessary condition of the National defence during the French Revolution.

One might conclude by saying what might seem too good to be true: namely, that minute and accurate information upon details (the characteristic of our time in the science of history) must of its own nature so corroborate just and general judgments of the past, that through it, when the modern phase of wilful distortion is over, mere blind scholarship will restore tradition.

I say it sounds too good to be true. But three or four examples of such action are already before us. Consider the Gospel of St. John, for instance, or what is called " the Higher Criticism " of the old Hebrew literature, and ask yourselves whether modern scholarship has not tended to restore the long and sane judgment of men, which, when that scholarship was still imperfect, seemed to imperil.

XXXIV

THE HIGHER CRITICISM

I HAVE long desired to make some protest against the attitude which the Very Learned take to·~ards literary evidence. I know that the Very Learned chop and change. I know that they are in this country about fifty years behind the Continent. I know that their devotion to the extraordinary unintelligent German methods will soon be shaken by their discovery that new methods are abroad—in both senses of the word " abroad ": for new methods have been abroad, thank Heaven, for a very long time.

But I also know that a mere appeal to reason will be of very little use, so I propose here to give a concrete instance, and I submit it to the judgment of the Very Learned.

The Very Learned when they desire to fix the date or the authenticity or both of a piece of literature, adopt among other postulates, these:

THE HIGHER CRITICISM

(1) That tradition doesn't count.

(2) That common sense, one's general knowledge of the time, and all that multiplex integration which the same mind effects from a million tiny data to a general judgment, is too tiny to be worthy of their august consideration.

(3) That the title " Very Learned " (which gives them their authority) is tarnished by any form of general knowledge and can only be acquired by confining oneself to a narrow field in which any fool could become an absolute master in about two years.

These are their negative postulates in dealing with a document.

As to their positive methods, of one hundred insufficient tricks I choose in particular these:

(1) The establishment of the date of the document against tradition and general air, by allusion discovered within it.

(2) The conception that all unusual events recorded in it are mythical, and therefore necessarily anterior to the document.

THE HIGHER CRITICISM

(3) The supposition that religions emotion, or indeed emotion of any kind, vitiates record.

(4) The admission of a single piece of corelative documentary evidence to destroy the reader's general judgment.

(5) The fixed dogma that most writers of the past have spent most of their time in forging.

Now to test these nincompoops I will consider a contemporary document which I know a good deal about, called *The Path to Rome.* It professes to be the record of a journey by one H. Belloc in the year 1901 from Toul in Lorraine to Rome in Italy. I will suppose that opus to have survived through some accident into a time which preserved few contemporary documents, but which had, through tradition and through a knowledge of surrounding circumstance, a popular idea of what the opening of the twentieth century was like, and a pathetic belief that Belloc had taken this journey in the year 1901.

THE HIGHER CRITICISM

This is how the Very Learned would proceed to teach the vulgar a lesson in scepticism.

" A critical examination of the document has confirmed me in the conclusion that the so-called *Path to Rome* is composed of three distinct elements, which I will call A, W, and θ." (See my article E.H.R., September 3, 113, pp. 233 *et seq.* for θ. For W, see Furth in Die Quellen Critik, 2nd Semestre, 3117.)

Of these three documents A is certainly much earlier than the rather loose criticism of Polter in England and Bergmann upon the Continent decided some years ago in the Monograph of the one, and the Discursions which the other has incorporated in his *Neo-Catholicism in the Twenty-Second Century.*

The English scholar advances a certain inferior limit of A.D. 2208, and a doubtful superior limit of A.D. 2236. The German is more precise and fixes the date of A in a year certainly lying between 2211 and 2217. I need not here recapitulate the well-known arguments with which this view is supported (See Z.M. fs.

THE HIGHER CRITICISM

(Mk. 2) Arch. and the very interesting article of my friend Mr. Gouch in the Pursuits of the A.S.) I may say generally that their argument reposes upon two considerations:

(1) The *Centime*, a coin which is mentioned several times in the book, went out of circulation before the middle of the twenty-first century, as we know from the only extant letter (undoubtedly genuine) of Henri Perro to the Prefect of Aude.

This gives them their superior limit. But it is the Inferior Limit which concerns us most, and here the argument reposes upon one phrase. (Perkins' edition, p.   .) This phrase is printed in italics, and runs, " *Deleted by the Censor.*"

It is advanced that we know that a censorship of books was first established in America (where, as I shall show, *The Path to Rome* was written) in the year 2208, and there is ample evidence of the fact that no such institution was in actual existence before the twenty-second century in the English-speaking countries, though there is mention of it elsewhere in the twenty-first, and a fragment of the twentieth appears to allude to something of the kind in Russia at that time. (Baker has confused the Censorship of *Books* with that of *Plays*, and an unknown form of art called " Morum " ; probably a species of private recitation.)

Now Dr. Blick has conclusively shown in his critical edition of the mass of ancient literature, commonly known as *The Statute Book*, that the use of italics is common to distinguish *later* interpolation.

This discovery is here of the first importance. Not only does it destroy the case for the phrase, " *Deleted by the Censor,*" as a proof of an Inferior Limit, 2208, but in this particular instance it is conclusive evidence that we have interpolation here, for it is obvious that *after* the establishment of a Censorship the right would exist to delete a name in the text, and a contemporary Editor would warn the reader in the fashion which he has, as a fact, employed.

So much for the negative argument. We

can be certain after Dr. Blick's epoch-making discovery that even the year 2208 is not our Inferior Limit for A, but we have what is much better, conclusive evidence of a much earlier *Superior* Limit, to which I must claim the modest title of discoverer.

There is a passage in A (pp. 170-171) notoriously corrupt, in which a dramatic dialogue between three characters, the Duchess, Major Charles and Clara, is no longer readable. All attempts to reconstitute it have failed, and on that account scholars have too much tended to neglect it.

Now I submit that though the passage is hopelessly corrupt its very corruption affords us a valuable indication.

The Duchess, in a stage indication, is made to address " Major Charles." It is notorious that the term " Major " applied to a certain functionary in a religious body probably affiliated to the Jesuits, known to modern scholars under a title drawn from the only contemporary fragment concerning it, as " Old Booth's

THE HIGHER CRITICISM

Ramp." This society was suppressed in America in the year 2012, *and the United States were the last country in which it survived.*

No matter how correct, therefore, the text is in this passage, we may be certain that even the careless scribe took the contemporary existence of a " major " for granted. And we may be equally certain that even our existing version of A incorporated in the only text we possess, was not written later than the first years of the twenty-first century. We have here, therefore, a new superior limit of capital importance, but, what is even more important, we can fix with fair accuracy a new inferior limit as well.

In the Preface (whose original attachment to A is undoubted) we have the title " Captain Monologue," p. XII (note again the word " Captain," an allusion to " Booth's Ramp," and in an anonymous fragment (B.M. m.s.s., 336 N., (60)), bearing the title, " Club Gossip," I have found the following conclusive sentence: " He used to bore us stiff, and old Burton invented a brand new title for him, ' Captain

Monologue,' about a year before he died, which the old chap did an hour or two after dinner on Derby Day."

Now this phrase is decisive. We have several allusions to " dinner " (in all, eight, and a doubtful ninth, tabulated by Ziethen in his *Corpus. Ins. Am.*). They all refer to some great public function the exact nature of which is lost, but which undoubtedly held a great place in political life. At what intervals this function occurred we cannot tell, but the coincident allusion to Derby Day settles it.

The only Lord Derby canonized by the Church died in 1960 and the promulgation of Beatification (the earliest date that would permit the use of the word " day " for this Saint) was issued by Pope Urban XV in May, 2003. It is, therefore, absolutely certain that A was written at some time between the years 2003 to 2012. Nearer than that I do not profess to fix it; but I confess that the allusion (p. 226) to drinking coffee coupled with the corresponding allusion to drinking coffee in a license issued

THE HIGHER CRITICISM

for a Lockhart's Restaurant in 2006 inclines me to that precise year as the year in which A appeared, or at any rate was written.

I think in the above I have established the date of A beyond dispute.

I have no case to bring forward of general conclusions, and I know that many scholars will find my argument, however irrefutable, disturbing, for it is universally admitted that excluding the manifestly miraculous *Episodes of the Oracle, The Ointment of Epinal, The View of the Alps over a Hundred Miles*, etc., which are all of them properly referred to in **W.** and *θ* respectively, A itself contains numerous passages too closely connected with the text to be regarded as additions, yet manifestly legendary —such as the perpetual allusions to spirits, and in particular to a spirit called " Devil," the inordinate consumption of wine, the gift of tongues, etc. etc. But I submit that a whole century, especially in a time which pullulated with examples of credulity, such as the " Flying Men," " The Telephone," " Wireless Telegraphy," etc., is ample to allow for the growth of these mythical features.

I take it, therefore, as now established, that A in its entirety is not later than 2012 and probably as early as 2006. Upon W I cannot yet profess to have arrived at a decision, but I incline to put it at about forty years later, while θ (which includes most of the doggerel and is manifestly in another style, and from another hand) is admitted to be at least a generation later than " W " itself.

In a further paper I shall discuss the much-disputed point of authorship, and I shall attempt to show that Belloc, though the subject of numerous accretions, was a real historical figure, and that the author of A may even have worked upon fragments preserved by oral tradition from the actual conversation of that character.

That is how the damned fools write: and with brains of that standard Germans ask me to deny my God.

XXXV

THE FANATIC

"I asked Old Biggs (as the Duke of Racton used to be called) what he thought of Charlie Wilson. Old Biggs answered, 'Man like that's one of two things: a *Fanatic* or a *Fanatic*.' I thought this very funny."—*St. Germans Sporting Memoirs*, Vol. II, p. 186.

THIS is a kind of man whom we all love and yet all desire to moderate. He is excessive only in good, but his excess therein is dangerous. He proceeds from less to more; first irritated, then exasperated, then mad. He will not tolerate the necessary foibles of mankind. No, nor even their misunderstandings. He himself commonly takes refuge in some vice or other, but a small one, and from this bastion defends himself against all comers.

The Fanatic will exaggerate the operations of war. If it be necessary in the conquest of a province to murder certain women, he will cry shame blindly, without consideration of

martial conditions or remembrance that what
we do in war is absolved by indemnities there-
after following. It is the same with the death
of children in warfare, whether these be
starved to death in concentration camps or
more humanely spitted, or thrown down wells,
or dealt with in some other fashion, such as
the braining of them against walls and gate-
posts: nothing will suit the Fanatic in these
matters but a complete and absolute absten-
tion from them, without regard to strategy
or tactics or any other part of military science.
Now many a man shall argue against practices
of one sort or another, as against excesses.
But the Fanatic is nothing so reasonable,
being bound by a law of his nature or
rather a lack of law, to violent outburst
with no restraint upon it, and to impotent
gnashings.

It is so also in affairs of State when peace
reigns, for the Fanatic is for ever denouncing
what all men know must be and making
of common happenings an uncommon crime.

THE FANATIC

Thus, when a minister shall borrow of a money-lender certain sums which this last generously puts before him without condition or expense, what must your Fanatic do, but poke and pry into the whole circumstance, and when the usurer has his just reward, and is made a Peer to settle our laws for us, the Fanatic will go vainly about from one newspaper to another seeking which shall print his foolish " protest " (as he calls it). Mark you also that the Fanatic is quite indifferent to this: that his foolishness is of no effect. He will roar in an empty field as loud as any bull and challenge all men to meet him, and seems well pleased whether they come or no.

It is of the fanatical temper to regard some few men as heroes, or demigods, and then again, these having failed in something, to revile them damnably. Thus by the old religious sort you will find the Twelve Apostles in the Gospel very foolishly revered and made much of as though they were so many Idols, but let one of these (Judas to wit) show statesmanship and a manly sense, and Lord! how the Fanatic does rail at him!

So it is also with foreign nations. The Fanatic has no measure there and speaks of them as though they were his province, seeing that it is of his essence never to comprehend diversity of circumstance or measure. Thus our cousins oversea will very properly burn alive the negroes that infest them in those parts, and their children and young people will, when the negro has been thus despatched, collect his bones or charred clothing to keep the same in their collections, which later they compare one with another. This is their business not ours, and has proved in the effect of great value to their commonwealth. But the Fanatic will have none of it. To hear him talk you might imagine himself a negro or one that had in his own flesh tasted the fire, and in his rage he will blame one man and another quite indiscriminately: now the good President of these people (Mr. Roosevelt as he once was), now the humble instrument of justice who should have put a match to the African. And all this without the least consideration of those surrounding things and haps which made such dealing with negroes a very necessary thing.

There is nothing workable or of purpose in what this man does. He is for ever quarrelling with other men for their lack of time or memory or even courtesy to himself, for on this point he is very tender. He wearies men with repeating to them their own negotiations, as though these were in some way disgraceful. Thus if a man has taken a sum of money in order to write of the less pleasing characters of his mother; or if he has sold his vote in Parliament, or if he has become for his own good reasons the servant of some one weathier than he, or if he has seen fit to deal with the enemies of his country, the Fanatic will blurt out and blare such a man's considered action, hoping, it would seem, to have some support in his mere raving at it. But this he never gets, for mankind in the lump is too weighty and reasonable to accept any such wildness.

THE FANATIC

There is no curing the Fanatic, neither with offers of Money nor with blows, nor is there any method whatsoever of silencing him, save imprisonment, which, in this country, is the method most commonly taken. But in the main there is no need to act so violently by him, seeing that all men laugh at him for a fool and that he will have no man at his side. Commonly, he is of no effect at all, and we may remain his friend though much contemptuous of him, since contempt troubles him not at all. But there are moments, and notably in the doubt of a war, when the Fanatic may do great ill indeed. Then it is men's business to have him out at once and if necessary to put him to death, but whether by beheading, by hanging, or by crucifixion it is for sober judges to decide.

The Irish are very fanatical, and have driven from their country many landlords formerly wealthy who were the support and mainstay of all the island. It may be seen in Ireland how fanaticism can impoverish. Upon the other hand, the people of the Mile End Road and round by the north into Hackney Downs and so southward and westward into the City of London by Houndsditch are not fanatical at all, and enjoy for their reward an abounding prosperity.

XXXVI

A LEADING ARTICLE

AFTER the failure of the numerous conferences which have been held between Charles Stuart and the Commissioners of Parliament, and after a trial in Westminster Hall the incidents of which it would be painful to recall, the Court appointed for the purpose has reached a conclusion with which we think the mass of Englishmen will, however reluctantly, agree. The courtesy and good feeling upon which we pride ourselves in our political life seem to have been strangely forgotten during the controversies of the last few months. It would be invidious to name particular instances, and we readily admit that the circumstances were abnormal. Feeling ran high, and with Englishmen at least, who are accustomed to call a spade a spade, strong words will follow upon strong emotions; but we can hope that the final decision of the

A LEADING ARTICLE

Court will have put behind us for ever one of the most critical periods of discussion, with all its deplorable excesses and wild and whirling words, which we can remember in modern times.

Upon the principle of the conclusion to which the Court has come there is a virtual unanimity. Men as different as Colonel Harrison on the one hand and Mr. Justice Bradshaw on the other, Mr. Cromwell—whom surely all agree in regarding as a representative Englishman—and that very different character, Mr. Ireton, whom we do not always agree with, but who certainly stands for a great section of opinion, are at one upon a policy which has received no serious criticism, and recommends itself even to such various social types as the blunt soldier, Colonel Pride, and the refined aristocrat, Lord Grey of Groby.

But though a matter of such supreme importance to the mass of the people, a measure which it is acknowledged will bring joy to the joyless, light to those who sit in darkness, and a new hope in their old age to fifteen millions

A LEADING ARTICLE

of British working men and women, may be unanimously agreed to in principle, it is unfortunately possible to defeat even so beneficent a measure by tactics of delay and by a prolonged criticism upon detail. The Government have therefore, in our opinion, acted wisely in determining to proceed with due expedition to the execution of Charles Stuart, and we do not anticipate any such resistance, even partial and sporadic, as certain rash freelances of politics have prophesied. There was indeed some time ago some doubt as to the success of a policy to which the Government was pledged, and in spite of the strong and disciplined majority which they commanded in the House, in spite of the fact that the House was actually unanimous upon the general lines of that policy, many people up and down the country, who did not fully comprehend it, had been led to act rashly and even riotously against its proposals. All that we may fairly say is now over, and we trust that the Government will have the firmness to go forward with a piece of work in which it now undoubtedly has the support of every class of society.

We should be the last to deny the importance of meeting any serious objection in detail that still remains. Thus the inhabitants of Charing Cross have a legitimate grievance when they say that the scene of the execution will be hidden from them by the brick building which stands at the northern end of Whitehall, but they must remember that all practical measures involve compromise and that if their point of view alone had been considered and the scaffold were to be erected upon the north of that annex, the crowd for which the Home Secretary has made such wise provision by the erection of strong temporary barriers in the Court of the Palace would have no chance of attending at the ceremony.

We confess that the more serious point seems to us to arise on the Bishop of London's suggestion that only the clergy of the Established Church should be present upon the platform, and we very much fear that this pretension—

317

A LEADING ARTICLE

in our view a very narrow and contemptible one—will receive the support of that large number of our fellow citizens which is still attached to the Episcopal forms of Christianity. But we take leave to remind them, and the Bishop of London himself, that the present moment, when the Free Churches have so fully vindicated their rights to public recognition, is hardly one in which it is decent to press these old-fashioned claims of privilege.

There is a third matter which we cannot conclude without mentioning: we refer to the attitude of Charles Stuart himself. While the matter was still *sub judice* we purposely refrained from making any comment, as is the laudable custom, we are glad to say, in the country. But now the sentence has been pronounced we think it our duty to protest against the attitude of Charles Stuart during the last scene of this momentous political controversy. He is too much of an English gentleman and statesman to exaggerate the significance of our criticism, or to fail to understand the spirit in which it is offered, for that is entirely friendly, but he must surely recognise by this time, that such petty ebullitions of temper as he exhibited in refusing to plead and in wearing his hat in the presence of men of such eminence as Mr. Justice Bradshaw were unworthy of him and of the great cause which he represents. He would have done well to take a lesson from the humble tipstaff of the Court, who, though not required to do so by the Judges, instantly removed his cap when they appeared and only put it on again when he was conducting the prisoner back after the rising of Court.

Finally, we hope that all those who have been permitted by the Home Secretary to be present at Whitehall upon next Tuesday will remember our national reputation for sobriety and judgment in great affairs of the State, and will be guilty of nothing that might make it necessary for the Government to use severe measures utterly repugnant to the spirit of English liberty.

XXXVII

THE OBITUARY NOTICE

Mr. Herod, whose death has just been announced by a telegram from Lyons, was one of the most striking and forceful personalities of our time.

By birth he was a Syrian Jew, suffering from the prejudice attaching to such an origin, and apparently with little prospect of achieving the great place which he did achieve in the eager life of our generation.

But his indomitable energy and his vast comprehension of men permitted him before the close of his long and useful life to impress himself upon his contemporaries as very few even of the greatest have done.

Our late beloved sovereign, Tiberius, perhaps the keenest judge of men in the whole Empire, is said to have remarked one evening in the smoking-room to his guests, when Herod had but recently left the apartment: "Gentlemen, that man is the corner-stone of my Eastern policy," and the tone in which His Majesty expressed this opinion was, we may be sure, that not only of considered judgment, but of equally considered reverence and praise.

It is a striking testimony to Mr. Herod's character that while he was still quite unknown (save, of course, as the heir of his father) he mastered the Greek and Latin tongues, and we find in his diary the shrewd remark that as the first was necessary to culture, so was the second to statesmanship.

It would have been impossible to choose a more difficult moment than that in which the then unknown Oriental lad was entrusted by the Imperial Government with the task which he has so triumphantly accomplished. The Levant, as our readers know, presents problems of peculiar difficulty, and though we can hardly doubt that the free and democratic genius of our country would at last have solved them, we owe it to the memory of this remarkable personality that the solution of them should have been so triumphantly successful.

We will not here recapitulate the obscure and often petty intrigues which have combined to give the politics of Judæa and its neighbourhood a character of anarchy. It is enough to point out that when Mr. Herod was first entrusted with his mission the gravest doubts were entertained as to whether the cause of order could prevail. The finances of the province were in chaos, and that detestable masquerade of enthusiasm to which the Levantines are so deplorably addicted, especially on their " religious " side, had baffled every attempt to re-establish order.

Mr. Herod's father (to whom it will be remembered the Empire had entrusted the beginnings of this difficult business), though undoubtedly a great man, had incurred the hatred of all the worst and too powerful forces of disorder in the district. His stern sense of justice and his unflinching resolution in one of the last affairs of his life, when he had promulgated his epoch-making edict to regulate the infantile death-rate—a scientific measure grossly misunderstood and unfortunately resented by the populace—had left a peculiarly difficult inheritance to the son. The women of the lower classes (as is nearly always the case in these social reforms) proved the chief obstacle, and legends of the most fantastic character were—and still are—current in the slums of Tiberias with regard to Mr. Herod Senior. When, some years later, he was struggling with a painful disease which it needed all his magnificent strength of character to master, no sympathy was shown him by the provincials of the Tetrarchy, and, to their shame be it said, the professional and landed classes treasonably lent the weight of their influence to the disloyal side.

It was therefore under difficulties of no common order that Mr. A. Herod, the son, took over the administration of that far border province which, we fear, will cause more trouble before its unruly inhabitants are absorbed in the mass of our beneficent and tolerant imperial system.

As though his public functions were not burden enough for such young shoulders to bear, the statesman's private life was assailed in the meanest and most despicable fashion. His marriage with Mrs. Herodias Philip—to whose lifelong devotion and support Mr. Herod bore such beautiful witness in his dedication of *Stray Leaves from Galilee*—was dragged into the glare of publicity by the less reputable demagogues of the region, causing infinite pain and doing irreparable injury to a most united and sensitive family circle. The hand of the law fell heavily upon more than one of the slanderers, but the evil was done, and Mr. Herod's authority, in the remote country districts, especially, was grievously affected for some years.

Through all these manifold obstacles Mr. Herod found or drove a way, and finally achieved the position we all look back to with such gratitude and pride in the really dangerous crisis which will be fresh in our readers' memory. It required no ordinary skill to pilot the policy of the Empire through those stormy three days in Jerusalem, but Mr. Herod was equal to the task, and emerged from it permanently established in the respect and affection of the Roman people. It is a sufficient testimony to his tact and firmness on this occasion that he earned in that moment of danger the lasting friendship and regard of Sir Pontius Pilate, whose firmness of vision and judgment of men were inferior only to that of his lamented sovereign.

Unlike most non-Italians and natives generally, Mr. Herod was an excellent judge of horseflesh, and his stables upon Mount Carmel often carried to victory the colours—*rose tendre*—of " Sir Caius Gracchus," the *nom-de-guerre* by which the statesman preferred to be known on the Turf.

Mr. Herod's æsthetic side was more highly developed than is commonly discovered in level-headed men of action. He personally supervised the architectural work in the rebuilding of Tiberias, and, of the lighter arts, was a judge of dramatic or " expressional " dancing.

During the earlier years of this eventful career Mr. Herod's life was greatly cheered and brightened by the companionship of his stepdaughter, Miss Salome Philip (now Lady Caiaphas), whose brilliant *salon* so long adorned the Quirinal, and who—we are exceedingly glad to hear—has been entrusted with that labour of love, the editing of her stepfather's life, letters, and verses; for Mr. Herod was no mean poet, and we may look forward with pleasurable expectation to his hitherto unpublished elegiacs on the beautiful scenery of his native land.

By the provisions of Mr. Herod's will he is to be cremated, and the ceremony will take place on a pyre of cedar-wood in the Place Bellecour at Lyons.

XXXVIII

THE "MERRY ROME" COLUMN

A weekly feature of the *Carthaginian Messenger*, quoted
from its issue of March 15, 220 B. C.

IT is quite a pleasure to be in dear old Rome
again after a week spent upon an important
mission which your readers are already acquainted with, in the Tuscan country. All
that drive through Etruria was very delightful
and the investigation will undoubtedly prove
of the greatest use. But what a difference it
is to be back in the sparkle and gaiety of the
Via Sacra. Every day one feels more and
more how *real* the entente is. Probably no nations have become faster friends than those
who have learnt to respect each other in war,
and though the Romans were compelled to accept our terms, and to undertake the difficult
administration of Sicily with money furnished
by the Carthaginian Government, all that was

more than twenty years ago and the memory of it does not rankle now. Indeed, I think I may say that the Roman character is a peculiarly generous one in this regard. They know what a good fight is, and they enjoy it—none better —but when it is over no one is readier to shake hands and to make friends again than a Roman. I was talking it over with dear little Lucia Balba the other day and I thought she put it very prettily. She said:

Est autem amicitia nihil aliud, nisi omnium divinarum huminarumque rerum cockalorumque Romanorum et jejorum concinnatio!

Was it not charming?

Of course there is a little jealousy—no more than a pout!—about Hasdrubal's magnificent work in Spain, but every one recognises what a great man he is, and it was only yesterday that M. Catulus (the son of our fine old enemy Lutatius) said to me with a sigh: " The reason we Romans cannot do that kind of thing is because we cannot stick together. We are for ever fighting among ourselves. Just look at our history!" On the other hand, I can't think that our mixture of democracy and common sense would suit the Latin temperament, with its *verve* and *nescio quid,* which make it at the same time so incalculable and so fascinating. Every nation must have its own advantages and drawbacks. We are a little too stolid, perhaps, and a little too businesslike, but our stolidity and our businesslike capacity have founded Colonies over the whole world and established a magnificent Empire. The Romans are a little too fond of " glory " and give way to sudden emotion in a fashion which seems to us perilously like weakness, but no one can deny that they have established a wonderfully methodical and orderly system of roads all over Italy, and that their capital is still the intellectual centre of the world.

Talking of that I ought to pay a tribute to the Roman home and to Roman thrift. We hear too much in our country of the Roman amphitheatre and all the rest of it. What many Carthaginians do not yet know is that the stay-at-home sober Roman is the backbone of the whole place. He hates war as heartily as we do, and though his forms of justice are very different from ours he is a sincere lover of right-dealing according to his lights. It is due to such men that Rome is, after ourselves, the chief financial power in the world.

But you will ask me for more interesting news than this sermon. Well! Well! I have plenty to give you. The Debates in the Senate are as brilliant and, I am afraid, as theatrical as usual. Certainly the Romans beat us at oratory. To hear Flaccus deliver a really great speech about the introduction of Greek manners is a thing one can never forget! Of course, it will seem to you in Carthage very unpractical and very " Roman," and it is true that that kind of thing doesn't make a nation great in the way we have become great, but it is wonderful stuff to hear all the same—and such a young man too! The Senate has, however, none of our ideas of order, and the marvel is how they get through their work at all.

THE "MERRY ROME" COLUMN

There are no Suffetes, and sometimes you will hear five or six men all talking at once and gesticulating in that laughable Italian fashion which our caricaturists find so valuable!

Those of my readers who run over to Rome two or three times a year for the Games will be interested to·hear that the great Aurelian house near the New Temple of Saturn (the rogues with their " Temples!" But still there is a good deal of real religion left in Rome) is being pulled down and a splendid one is being put in its place upon the designs of a really remarkable young architect, Pneius Caius Agricola. He is the nephew, by the way, of Sopher Masher Baal, whom we all know so well at Carthage, and who is, I think, technically, a Carthaginian citizen. Possibly I am wrong, for I remember a delightful dinner with him years ago among our cousins overseas, and he may very possibly be Tyrian. If so, and if these humble lines meet his eye, I tender him my apologies. But anyhow, his nephew is a very remarkable and original artist whom all

THE "MERRY ROME" COLUMN

Rome is eager to applaud. When the new Aurelian House is finished it will have a façade in five orders, Doric, Ionic, Corinthian, heavy Egyptian on the fourth story, and Assyrian on the top, the whole terminating in a vast pyramid, which is to have the appearance of stone, but which will really be a light erection in thin plaster slabs.

Last Wednesday we had the review of the troops. You may imagine how the Roman populace delighted in *that!* There is a good deal that is old-fashioned to our ideas in the accouterments, and it was certainly comic to see an " admiral " leading his " sailors " past the saluting post like so many marines! But it is always a pleasant spectacle for a warm-hearted man to see the humbler classes of Rome picnicking in true Roman fashion upon the Campus Martius and cheering their sons and brothers. The army is very popular in Rome, although the men are paid hardly anything—a mere nominal sum. The Romans do not come up to our standard of physique, and I am afraid the Golden Legion would laugh at them. But they are sturdy little fellows, and not to be despised when it comes to marching, or turning their hands to the thousand domestic details of the camp; moreover, they are invariably good-humoured, and that is a great charm.

It is unfortunately impossible to officer all the troops with gentlemen, and that is a drawback of which thoughtful Romans are acutely conscious. It is on this account that there is none of that cordial relation between officer and man which we take for granted in our service. An intelligent and travelled Roman said to me the other day: "How I envy you your Carthaginian officers! Always in training! Always ready! Always urbane!" But we must remember that our service is not so numerous as theirs.

I must not ramble on further, for the post is going, and you know what the Roman post *is*. It starts when it feels inclined, and the delivery is *tantum quantum*, as we say in Italy. I have to be a good hour before the official time

THE "MERRY ROME" COLUMN

or risk being told by some shabbily uniformed person that my letter missed *through my own fault!* Next week I hope to give you an interesting account of Sapphira Moshetim's début. She is a Roman of the Romans, and I was quite carried away! Such subtlety! Such declamation! I hope to be her herald, for she is to come to Carthage next season, and I am sure she will bear out all I say.

XXXIX

OPEN LETTER TO A YOUNG PARASITE

My dear Boy:

As you know, I was your father's closest friend for many years, and I have watched with interest, but I confess not without anxiety, your first attempts in a career of which he was in my young days the most brilliant exemplar.

You will not take it ill in a man of my years and in one as devoted to your family as I am and have proved myself to be, if I tender you a word of advice.

The profession upon which you have engaged is one of the most difficult in the world. It does not offer the great prizes which attend the best forms of cheating, bullying, and blackmail, and at the same time it is highly limited, and offers opportunities to only a handful of the finer souls.

Nevertheless, I am not writing this to dissuade you for one moment from its pursuit. There is something in the fine arts difficult to define, but very deeply felt by every one, which makes them of themselves a sort of compensation for their economic limitations. The artist, the poet, and the actor expect to live, and hope to live well, but each one knows how few are the prizes, and each in his heart expects something more than a mere money compensation. So should it be in that great profession which you have undertaken in the light of your father's example.

In connection with that, I think it my duty to point out to you that even the greatest success in this special calling is only modest compared with successes obtained at the Bar, in commerce, or even in politics. You will never become a wealthy man. I do not desire it for you. It should be yours, if you succeed, to enjoy wealth without its responsibility, and to consume the good things our civilisation presents to the wealthy without avarice, without the memory of preceding poverty, and, above all, without the torturing necessity of considering the less fortunate of your kind.

You must not expect, my dear young man, to leave even a modest competence; therefore you must not expect to marry and provide for children. The parasite must be celibate. I have never known the rule to fail, at least in our sex. You will tell me, perhaps, that in the course of your career, continually inhabiting the houses of the rich, studying their manners, and supplying their wants, you cannot fail to meet some heiress; that you do not see why, this being the case, you should not marry her, to your lasting advantage.

Let me beg you, with all the earnestness in my power, to put such thoughts from you altogether. They are as fatal to a parasite's success as early commercial bargaining to that of a painter. You must in the first ten years of your exercises devote yourself wholly to your great calling. By the time you have done that you will have unlearned or forgotten all that goes with a wealthy marriage; its heavy responsibilities will be odious to you, its sense of dependence intolerable. Moreover (though you may think it a little cynical of me to say so), I must assure you that no one, even a man with your exalted ideal, can make a success of married life unless he enters it with some considerable respect for his partner. Now, it is easy for the man who lays himself out for a rich marriage (and that is a business quite different from your own, and one, therefore, on which I will not enter) to respect his wife. Such men are commonly possessed, or soon become possessed, of a simple and profound religion, which is the worship of money, and when they have found their inevitable choice, her substance, or that of her father, surrounds her with a halo that does not fade. You could hope for no such illusions. The very first year of your vocation (if you pursue it industriously and honestly) will destroy in you the possibility of any form of worship whatsoever. No, it will be yours to take up with dignity, and I trust in

TO A YOUNG PARASITE

some permanent fashion, that position of parasite which is a proper and necessary adjunct
in every wealthy family, and which, when it is
once well and industriously occupied, I have
never known to fail in promoting the happiness
of its incumbent.

Let me turn from all this and give you a
few rough rules which should guide you in
the earlier part of your way. You will not,
I am sure, reject them lightly, coming as they
do from a friend of my standing and experience. Young men commonly regard the advice of their elders as something too crude to
be observed. It is a fatal error. What they
take for crudity is only the terseness and
pressure of accumulated experience.

The first main rule is to take note of that
limit of insult and contempt beyond which your
master will revolt. Note carefully what I say.
No one, and least of all the prosperous, especially when their prosperity is combined with
culture, will long tolerate flattery. A certain
indifference, spiced with occasional contempt

and not infrequent insolence, is what those of jaded appetite look for in any permanent companion. Without a full knowledge of this great truth, hundreds of your compeers have fallen early upon the field, never to rise again. For if it is true that the wealthy and the refined demand much seasoning in their companionship, it is equally true that there is a fairly sharp boundary beyond which they suddenly revolt. Henry Bellarmine was thrust out of the Congletons' house for no other reason. The same cause led to poor Ralph Pagberry's imprisonment, and I could quote you hosts of others.

My next rule is that you should never, un ler any temptation of weather, or ill health, or fatigue, permit yourself really and thoroughly to bore either your patron or any one of his guests, near relatives, or advisers. As it is not easy for a young man to know when he is boring the well-to-do, let me give you a few hints.

When the rich begin to talk one to the other in your presence without noticing you, it is a sign. When they answer what you are saying to them in a manner totally irrelevant, it is another. When they smile very sympathetically, but at something else in the room, not your face, it is a third. And when they give an interested exclamation, such as, " No doubt. No doubt," or, " I can well believe it," such expressions having no relation to what passed immediately before, it is a fourth.

Add to these criteria certain plain rules, such as never upon any account to read aloud to the rich unless they constrain you to do so, never to sing, never to be the last to leave the room or to go to bed, and you will not sin upon this score.

Let me give you a further rule, which is, to agree with the women. It is very difficult for one of our sex to remember this, because our sex loves argument and is with difficulty persuaded that contradiction and even controversy are intolerable to ladies. Mould your conversation with them in such a fashion that they may hear from you either a brilliant account at second hand of themselves or a very odious

one of their friends; but do not be so foolish
as to touch upon abstract matters, and if these
by any chance fall into the conversation, simply
discover your companion's real or supposed
position, and agree with it.

I have little more to add. Be courteous to
all chance guests in the house. You will tell
me, justly enough, that the great majority of
them will be unimportant or poor or both. But
the point is that you can never tell when one
of them may turn out to be, either then or in
the future, important or rich or both. The
rule is simple and absolute. Cultivate courtesy,
avoid affection; use the first upon all occasions,
and forget so much as the meaning of the
second.

Lastly, drink wine, but drink it in modera-
tion. I have known admirably successful para-
sites who were total abstainers, but only in the
houses of fanatics with whom this peculiar habit
was a creed. The moment these successful men
passed to other employers, I was interested to
note that they at once abandoned the foolish

trick. But if it is important not to fall into the Mohammedan foible of total abstinence from wine, it is, if anything, even more important never upon any occasion whatsoever to exceed in it. Excess in wine is dangerous in a degree to the burglar, the thief, the money-lender, the poisoner, and many professions other than your own, but in that which you have chosen it is not *dangerous*, but *fatal*. Let such excess be apparent once in the career of a young parasite, and that career is as good as done for. I urge this truth upon you most solemnly, my dear lad, by way of ending.

I wish you the best of luck, and I am your poor father's devoted friend and your own.

XL

ON DROPPING ANCHOR

THE best noise in all the world is the rattle of
the anchor chain when one comes into harbour
at last, and lets it go over the bows.

You may say that one does nothing of the
sort, that one picks up moorings, and that letting go so heavy a thing as an anchor is no
business for you and me. If you say that you
are wrong. Men go from inhabited place to
inhabited place, and for pleasure from station
to station, then pick up moorings as best they
can, usually craning over the side and grab-
bing as they pass, and cursing the man astern
for leaving such way on her and for passing so
wide. Yes, I know that. You are not the only
man who has picked up moorings. Not by
many many thousands. Many moorings have
I picked up in many places, none without some

344

sort of misfortune; therefore do I still prefer the rattle of the anchor chain.

Once—to be accurate, seventeen years ago —I had been out all night by myself in a boat called the *Silver Star*. She was a very small boat. She had only one sail; she was black inside and out, and I think about one hundred years old. I had hired her of a poor man, and she was his only possession.

It was a rough night in the late summer when the rich are compelled in their detestable grind to go to the Solent. When I say it was night I mean it was the early morning, just late enough for the rich to be asleep aboard their boats, and the dawn was silent upon the sea. There was a strong tide running up the Medina. I was tired to death. I had passed the Royal Yacht Squadron grounds, and the first thing I saw was a very fine and noble buoy—new-painted, gay, lordly—moorings worthy of a man!

I let go the halyard very briskly, and I nipped forward and got my hand upon that

great buoy—there was no hauling of it in-
board; I took the little painter of my boat and
made it fast to this noble buoy, and then immediately I fell asleep. In this sleep of mine
I heard, as in a pleasant dream, the exact motion of many oars rowed by strong men, and
very soon afterwards I heard a voice with a
Colonial accent swearing in an abominable manner, and I woke up and looked—and there was
a man of prodigious wealth, all dressed in
white, and with an extremely new cap on his
head. His whiskers also were white and his
face bright red, and he was in a great passion.
He was evidently the owner or master of the
buoy, and on either side of the fine boat in which
he rowed were the rowers, his slaves. He could
not conceive why I had tied the *Silver Star* to
his magnificent great imperial moorings, to
which he had decided to tie his own expensive
ship, on which, no doubt, a dozen as rich as himself were sailing the seas.

I told him that I was sorry I had picked up
his moorings, but that, in this country, it was

the common courtesy of the sea to pick up any spare moorings one could find. I also asked him the name of his expensive ship, but he only answered with curses. I told him the name of my ship was the *Silver Star*.

Then, when I had cast off, I put out the sweeps and I rowed gently, for it was now slack water at the top of the tide, and I stood by while he tied his magnificent yacht to the moorings. When he had done that I rowed under the stern of that ship and read her name. But I will not print it here, only let me tell you it was the name of a ship belonging to a fabulously rich man. Riches, I thought then and I think still, corrupt the heart.

Upon another occasion I came with one companion across the bar of Orford River, out of a very heavy wind outside and a very heavy sea. I just touched as I crossed that bar, though I was on the top of the highest tide of the year, for it was just this time in September, the highest springs of the hunter's moon.

My companion and I sailed up Orford River,

and when we came to Orford Town we saw a buoy, and I said to my companion, " Let us pick up moorings."

Upon the bank of the river was a long line of men, all shouting and howling, and warning us not to touch that buoy. But we called out to them that we meant no harm. We only meant to pick up those moorings for a moment, so as to make everything snug on board, and that then we would take a line ashore and lie close to the wharf. Only the more did those numerous men (whom many others ran up to join as I called) forbid us with oaths to touch the buoy. Nevertheless, we picked up the little buoy (which was quite small and light) and we got it in-board, and held on, waiting for our boat to swing to it. But an astonishing thing happened! The boat paid no attention to the moorings, but went careering up river carrying the buoy with it, and apparently dragging the moorings along the bottom without the least difficulty. And this was no wonder, for we found out afterwards that the little buoy had only been set there to mark a racing point, and that the weights holding the line of it to the bottom were very light and few. So it was no wonder the men of Orford had been so angry. Soon it was dark, and we replaced the buoy stealthily, and when we came in to eat at the Inn we were not recognised.

It was on this occasion that was written the song:

> The men that lived in Orford stood
> Upon the shore to meet me;
> Their faces were like carven wood,
> They did not wish to greet me.
> etc.

It has eighteen verses.

I say again, unless you have moorings of your own—an extravagant habit—picking up moorings is always a perilous and doubtful thing, fraught with accident and hatred and mischance. Give me the rattle of the anchor chain!

I love to consider a place which I have never yet seen, but which I shall reach at last, full of repose and marking the end of those voyages, and security from the tumble of the sea.

This place will be a cove set round with high hills on which there shall be no house or sign of men, and it shall be enfolded by quite deserted land; but the westering sun will shine pleasantly upon it under a warm air. It will be a proper place for sleep.

The fair-way into that haven shall lie behind a pleasant little beach of shingle, which shall run out aslant into the sea from the steep hillside, and shall be a breakwater made by God. The tide shall run up behind it smoothly, and in a silent way, filling the quiet hollow of the hills, brimming it all up like a cup—a cup of refreshment and of quiet, a cup of ending.

Then with what pleasure shall I put my small boat round, just round the point of that shingle beach, noting the shoal water by the eddies and the deeps by the blue colour of them where the channel runs from the main into the fair-way. Up that fair-way shall I go, up into the cove, and the gates of it shall shut behind me, headland against headland, so that I shall not see the open sea any more, though I shall still hear its distant noise. But all around me, save for that distant echo of the surf from the high hills, will be silence; and the evening will be gathering already.

Under that falling light, all alone in such a place, I shall let go the anchor chain, and let it rattle for the last time. My anchor will go down into the clear salt water with a run, and when it touches I shall pay out four lengths or more so that she may swing easily and not drag, and then I shall tie up my canvas and fasten all for the night, and get me ready for sleep. And that will be the end of my sailing.